# GOSPEL INSIGHTS FOR
## *Everyday Living*

# Dedication

To Robert and Chris Brown—lifelong friends who help me remember and keep me laughing whenever I've needed it.

# Acknowledgments

A book is never the work of one person. My family has not only given me experiences to write about, but suffered through my musings (they call it preaching!) for years. Because of this, many thanks go to Boyd and Laresa Campbell, Jay Dee and Talena Kerr, David and Breana Tilley, Brent and Anissa Olsen, Michael and Mariah Wickham, Morgan and Kirsha Quigley, Daniel and Meleah Ferguson, Nick and Patrea Heath, and Joshua and Jackie Johnson for all they have taught me and for their patience. In addition, I'm grateful to Sonoma, from whom I learned so much even though she died at birth.

I am also thankful for the women I exercised with while this book was being written. They let me talk through principles I was trying to put into words, and they listened while I thought out loud. They gave me valuable feedback and urged me on when the struggle to write became discouraging. I owe much to Sue Ellen Call, Kathy Hill, Sharon Biegler, Michelle Golightly, Lynda Taylor, Sue Clearwater, Jackie Williamson, Lila Tueller, Holly Fowler, and Melanie Power.

Of course, I am grateful to Leatherwood for publishing my book and to Amy Orton and Linda Prince for their hard work in bringing it into being.

But most of all I'm thankful for my husband, Carl M. Johnson, who inspires me, cheers me on, and loves me despite my many failings.

# GOSPEL INSIGHTS FOR
## *Everyday Living*

### SHERRIE MILLS JOHNSON

# Introduction

One day while I was exercising with a friend, she expressed her desire to study the gospel in more detail. "I study my scriptures," she said, "but I don't always get it. I need someone to explain it to me." She then went on to complain that she often saw big, "academic-type" books that discuss gospel principles, but while caring for her large family she didn't have the time or the energy to sit down and read such books. "I wish you'd write a book," she said, "that discusses gospel principles in short chapters I can read in little snatches of time between carpools."

*Gospel Insights for Everyday Living* is the result of that conversation. But as I started on the book, I realized that there was another benefit to talking about gospel principles one at a time in short chapters. Progressing in the gospel isn't just about learning new things. It is about remembering and rejoicing in the good news that is the plan of salvation. It is about, on a daily basis, filling our hearts and then dwelling on all that is good. Therefore, even if we already understand gospel principles, there is joy and enlightenment that comes from reviewing them. As my insights spark your own insights, it gives you more to ponder and delight in. The intent is not to include every gospel principle or even all the aspects of the principles discussed, but rather to provide a springboard for your own thinking.

That is why this book was written—to explore and review the gospel of Jesus Christ, one joyful insight at a time.

# Good News

*This is the gospel, the glad tidings, which the voice out of the heavens bore record unto us—That he came into the world, even Jesus, to be crucified for the world, and to bear the sins of the world, and to sanctify the world, and to cleanse it from all unrighteousness.*

Doctrine and Covenants 76:40

**Well was it said of old, 'Where there is no vision, the people perish' (Prov. 29:18). There is no place in this work for those who believe only in the gospel of doom and gloom. The gospel is good news. It is a message of triumph. It is a cause to be embraced with enthusiasm.**

Gordon B. Hinckley, "Stay the Course—Keep the Faith," *Ensign*, Nov. 1995, 70

We mortals complicate life unnecessarily. The gospel is meant to make life simpler, but the adversary does a very good job of obscuring that fact.

The word *gospel* comes to us from the Latin word *evangelium*, which is a compound of *eus*, meaning "good," and *angelos*, meaning "messenger." The word came into the English language as *gód spel*, or "good tidings," referring to the good tidings of angels or messengers. However, when the phrase came into English, only one "o" was used from the word *good*, leading to the mistaken interpretation that it was a compound word meaning "God's story." This may be an etymological error, but I personally think it makes sense. Any way you look at it, God's story is good news, and *the* good news is God's story.

The Doctrine and Covenants explains exactly what the good news is: "This is the gospel, the glad tidings, which the voice out of the heavens bore record unto us—That he came into the world, even Jesus, to be crucified for the world, and to bear the sins of the world, and to sanctify the world, and to cleanse it from all unrighteousness; That through him all might be saved whom the Father had put into his power and made by him" (D&C 76:41–42). What better news could there be? Because of Jesus Christ our fallen world can be sanctified, cleansed, and saved, and we with it!

When the Savior visited the Nephites, He told them, "Behold I have given unto you my gospel [good news], and this is the gospel [good news] which I have given unto you—that I came into the world to do the will of my Father, because my Father sent me. And my Father sent me that I might be lifted up upon the cross; and after that I had been lifted up upon the cross, that I might draw all men unto me, that as I have been lifted up by men even so should men be lifted up by the Father, to stand before me, to be judged of their works, whether they be good or whether they be evil" (3 Ne. 27:13–14).

One modern Apostle, Elder Jeffrey R. Holland, explained the good news this way: "The 'good news' was that death and hell could be escaped, that mistakes and sins could be overcome, that there was hope, that there was help, that the insoluble was solved, that the enemy had been conquered. The good news was that everyone's tomb could one day be empty, that everyone's soul could again be pure, that every child of God could again return to the Father who gave them life" (Jeffrey R. Holland, "Missionary Work and the Atonement," address given at the Provo [Utah] Missionary Training Center, 20 June 2000). Again, what better news could there be? Jesus Christ is our Savior. He can heal us. He will comfort us, calm us, teach us, and direct us back into the presence of God. But too often we let the vicissitudes of life get in the way of our happiness. We let the daily grind pulverize us instead of polish us. We forget the fact that there is good news, and we fill our minds with bad news.

Lehi tells us that "men are that they might have joy" (2 Ne. 2:25). Alma calls the gospel the "plan of happiness" (Alma 42:8). Happiness and joy are intended to be ours. The adversary relentlessly tries to keep us from understanding any of this by confusing the gospel with mortal life. He'd like us to think that the gospel is difficult and complicated and not at all enjoyable.

But gospel living is simple. The only requirement is that we do something good in the moment we are in. (And just as exciting as the simplicity of it all is the fact that there is so much good to choose from!) The bad that has happened in the past or whatever is looming in the future doesn't need to determine the present. God knows that we have no control over any moment but this present one, and He doesn't expect us to. We can't change the past and we can't force the future. All we need to worry about is right now, and God will take care of the rest.

The promises for those who center their attention and care in the present moment are out of this world, but we don't need to wait until the next life to reap the rewards. To those who concentrate on doing good, the promised blessings enrich their lives not only in the hereafter, but right now. As we are told in the Doctrine and Covenants, "Yea, blessed are they whose feet stand upon the land of Zion, who have obeyed my gospel; for they shall receive for their reward the good things of the earth, and it shall bring forth in its strength" (59:3).

The good news that is the gospel of Jesus Christ is that there is a solution to every failing, every mistake, every problem, every trial, every pain, every negative experience. That solution is Jesus Christ. As Elder Franklin D. Richards said, "Those who are seeking a plan of life that will bring them peace, relief from inner tensions, happiness, and growth and development will find it in the restored gospel of Jesus Christ" ("Justice, Mercy, and Humility," *Improvement Era,* June 1970, 37).

While we do live in a telestial world filled with pain, sorrow, adversity, anger, fatigue, and every other negative influence, Jesus Christ has promised, "These things I have spoken unto you, that in me ye might have peace. In the world ye shall have tribulation: but be of good cheer; I have overcome the world" (John 16:33). Indeed, that is very good news.

But if we are to take advantage of the peace, love, and joy that Jesus Christ offers, we must understand His teachings. He has instructed His followers, "Come unto me, all ye that labour and are heavy laden, and I will give you rest. Take my yoke upon you, and learn of me; for I am meek and lowly in heart: and ye shall find rest unto your souls. For my yoke is easy, and my burden is light" (Matt. 11:28–30). That is the best possible news! He lives. He cares. He heals. And the gospel has been preached to us so that we can learn of Him and partake of His peace.

# We Trusted Good Would Triumph

*Behold, the Lord shall come, and his*
*recompense shall be with him, and he shall reward*
*every man, and the poor shall rejoice.*

Doctrine and Covenants 56:19

**Along with knowing that God is there, it is equally vital to know what He is like, including His perfected attributes of justice and mercy. More mortals die in ignorance of God's true character than die in actual defiance of Him. Belief in the goodness and power of God is greatly facilitated by understanding His plan of salvation with its crucial allowance for mankind's moral agency, real moral agency—with real mistakes and with real consequences! His plan includes real tests, real dilemmas, real anguish, and real joy.**

Neal A. Maxwell, "Yet Thou Art There," *Ensign*, Nov. 1987, 30

I've often tried to imagine what Lucifer told the hosts of heaven as he tried to convince us that the great plan of salvation wouldn't work. What could Lucifer possibly have said in the very presence of God to discredit Him and convince a third-part of His children to follow him? While it is interesting to contemplate, the details of the debate are unknown. Nevertheless, I am sure that one of Lucifer's most convincing arguments centered on suffering. Certainly, he was quick to point out that if we were free to choose, some people would misuse their agency and hurt others. Innocent, good people—those who were endeavoring to do everything right so they could return home to Father—would suffer. Drunk drivers would maim and kill. Thieves and terrorists would ravish and destroy. Spouses, parents, and children would abuse the very people they were supposed to care for. Manipulative and conniving people would commit cruel and unjust acts for their own selfish gain and pleasure. Perhaps Lucifer gave examples—the kinds of things you and I read in the newspaper daily—and then invited us to consider, "Is this what you really want?"

When thought about in this way, our response is surprising. We agreed to the suffering! How we must have trusted our Heavenly Father and our Savior as They explained that mortal life would be difficult and painful, but that through the Atonement all injustice would be made right. Even our own acts of selfishness and sin would be overcome. We accepted the fact that God and Christ had the power to transcend the chaos of evil, selfishness, and terror, and that They would establish order, righteousness, and good. All we would have to do is endure, repent, and trust in Them. We believed that, as President James E. Faust stated, "In the eternal scheme of things, wrongs will be righted. In the perfect justice of the Lord, all who live worthily will be compensated for blessings not enjoyed here" (James E. Faust, "Hope, an Anchor of the Soul," *Ensign,* Nov. 1999, 59).

This principle was explained again to Adam and Eve in the garden. They were told that they could choose to live in Eden forever without pain and suffering, but that this choice would not allow them to progress. Their other choice was to eat of the tree of knowledge of good and evil and experience spiritual and physical death, which would bring pain and suffering into the world. Notice that there isn't a tree of only good and another tree of only evil. Good and evil come together in the same package—in the same fruit. To choose one is to choose the other.

Adam and Eve opted for the plan of good and evil. They partook of the fruit and changed the world. Committing the forbidden act was necessary in order to bring about a condition where evil could operate. In other words, it took an act of sin to introduce evil into the world. Like the preceding creative periods, it was good in that it brought about the opportunity to progress. But because of it Adam and Eve endured much pain and suffering. They toiled to produce food. They suffered to bring children into the world. They struggled to learn through the trial and error of their experiences. They cried over horrendous mistakes made by some of their children. They sorrowed at the discovery of what death really meant. They grew weary and exhausted and discouraged. But they didn't give up.

One of the great lessons that comes out of these stories of the premortal council and the Garden of Eden, is that good is not necessarily painless. In the beginning we understood that. The dividing line between good and evil is not the same line as the one that divides pleasure and pain or comfort and distress. Good is not always warm-fuzzy delightful.

We once saw through Lucifer's arguments and knew that pain was necessary. We trusted that our Heavenly Father and Jehovah had the power to save us from the bad and evil we would experience. But sometimes, since the veil has clouded our memories of that defining moment, we need to be reminded, as was Joseph Smith in one of his darkest moments, that "all these things shall give thee experience, and shall be for thy good" (D&C 122:7). God is great, and that greatness includes the power to consecrate all our afflictions for our gain. The word *consecrate* comes from Latin roots that mean "with holiness," and the English word means "dedicated to a sacred purpose." If we are faithful, all our afflictions will be dedicated to a sacred purpose—that of making us holy—by a loving God.

We once listened to and trusted our Father and our Savior enough to eagerly accept Their plan, which included pain and suffering. We knew it would be worth it. We knew They would make everything right in the end, if only we followed Them. Now, like Adam and Eve, we find ourselves in the throes of good and evil, but with confidence we can endure, for as the Savior has explained, "In the world ye shall have tribulation: but be of good cheer; I have overcome the world" (John 16:33).

# The Tree of Knowledge
# of Good and Evil

*Of every tree of the garden thou mayest*
*freely eat: But of the tree of the knowledge of good*
*and evil, thou shalt not eat of it: for in the day that*
*thou eatest thereof thou shalt surely die.*

Genesis 2:16–17

**We never tire of proclaiming the inspiring truth of the gospel that man is that he might have joy. For us the so-called fall of man placed the human spirit in a world of experience and adventure where evils are real but can be overcome, where free moral decision is a constant requirement, and where choices, freely made, determine the quality of life and the eventual condition of the soul.**

Hugh B. Brown, *Conference Report*, Apr. 1964, 82

In the Garden of Eden, only good existed. There were no thorns, no weeds, no toil, no sorrow, no burned fingers, no sprained ankles, no pain of any kind—not even guilty consciences. But neither Adam nor Eve knew how good they had it. Without experience with what is *not* good, without anything to compare good to, they had no knowledge. When we understand that they had good, but no knowledge of good, we realize that the most important element in the account is knowledge. That is why God sent us here—to gain knowledge of good and evil.

In order to progress, Adam and Eve had to gain knowledge—a very specific kind of knowledge. They needed to comprehend the difference between good and evil. To learn that difference they had to first be cut off from the presence of God, to experience spiritual death, because nothing evil can exist in God's presence (see Moses 6:57). After being separated from God's presence, they could experience evil and thereby come to know for themselves how it differs from good.

In the book of Moses, the account of God's instruction to Adam and Eve includes an important addition to this narrative. After telling them not to eat of the tree of knowledge of good and evil, God said, "Nevertheless, thou mayest choose for thyself, for it is given unto thee" (Moses 3:15). Since Adam and Eve could not experience evil in God's presence, they had a choice to make—a choice God could not make for them. They could stay forever in the garden, or they could break a commandment and thereby bring about evil so they could gain knowledge of good and evil. Only the second choice would allow them to progress so they could someday be like God. As Eve so aptly summarized it: "Were it not for our transgression we never should have had seed, and never should have known good and evil, and the joy of our redemption, and the eternal life which God giveth unto all the obedient" (Moses 5:11). Adam and Eve chose to gain knowledge, and because of their choice, we now get to make the same choice. Every day we make choices between good and evil that increase our knowledge. That is how we learn. That is how we progress: one choice at a time.

Because Adam and Eve chose to fall, we are born into a world where good and evil coexist, providing us with the opportunity to gain knowledge. And because Jesus Christ chose to break the death barriers created by the Fall, we have the opportunity to transcend evil. The choice is now ours. But unlike Adam and Eve, who had to choose whether or not to fall, our choice is whether or not to *rise*.

# Enmity

*I will put enmity between thee and the woman,*
*between thy seed and her seed; and he shall bruise thy*
*head, and thou shalt bruise his heel.*

Moses 4:21

**If we are not drawing towards God in principle, we are
going from Him and drawing towards the devil.**

Joseph Smith, *Teachings of the Prophet Joseph Smith*, comp. Joseph Fielding Smith
(Salt Lake City: Deseret Book Co., 1976), 216

For years I tried without success to make sense of God's command to place enmity between Satan and the seed of the woman. To me *enmity* meant hatred, and while I thought it might indicate that a sense of repulsion would exist between the two, I kept getting the feeling that I was missing the point. It did make a little more sense when I realized the "seed of the woman" referred to Jesus Christ. Satan would have power to bruise Christ's heel, but Christ would bruise, or as the Hebrew of the Genesis account states, Christ would have power to *crush* Satan's head. But I still didn't understand the enmity part.

Then one day I looked up the word *enmity* in the dictionary and found that it also means "a state of opposition." When God placed enmity in the world, He introduced "opposition in all things" (2 Ne. 2:11). This understanding gave me a visual picture. Enmity means that Christ and Satan exist at opposite ends of a line—opposed to one another.

Satan ———————————————————— Jesus Christ

I stand someplace along that line, and at any given moment I am either traveling toward Satan or toward Christ. Whenever I make a choice on this path, I choose amity with one and enmity with the other. It is impossible to do both at the same time. If I turn my back on Christ, I am facing Satan. If I turn my back on Satan, I am facing Christ. There are no perpendicular dissecting lines that allow me to walk another direction. At any given moment, I am either moving toward Christ or away from Him.

Some try to face Christ and walk backwards. That is called hypocrisy. Others try the opposite. They try to face Satan and walk backwards. This is called foolishness. It is not only flirting with danger, it is also extremely difficult to accomplish, because once you have turned toward Satan so that he is in your sight, his pull and enticement are very hard to overcome. Some claim that perhaps at the equidistant center point there exist "gray" areas. But as the visual diagram makes clear, there are only two choices: move toward Satan or move toward Christ. Enmity makes life a simple, two-way path.

When analyzed closely, a choice that appears to be gray is usually either a choice between two good things or a choice between two evil things. The comforting thought is that we are promised that the light of Christ will make all that is good known to us. Therefore, by the light of Christ we can know which choices we should make. As Mormon explains, "Behold, the Spirit of Christ is given to every man, that he may know good from evil" (Moroni 7:16). President Boyd K. Packer elaborated, "The Light of Christ is as universal as sunlight itself. Wherever there is human life, there is the Spirit of Christ. Every living soul is possessed of it. . . . It is the inspirer of everything that will bless and benefit mankind. It nourishes goodness itself (Boyd K. Packer, "The Light of Christ," *Ensign,* Apr. 2005, 13).

Isaiah explains what happens to people who refuse this radiant light and instead try to walk in the light they generate themselves. "Behold all ye that kindle a fire, that compass yourselves about with sparks: walk in the light of your fire, and in the sparks that ye have kindled. This shall ye have of mine hand; ye shall lie down in sorrow" (Isa. 50:11). The most light a mortal alone can generate is sparks. Therefore, the choice is to illuminate our way through the darkness of mortal life with the light generated by our own sparks, or to navigate by the brilliant light of Christ.

As people follow the light of Christ, they are led to the gospel, where they receive an increase in light: the gift of the Holy Ghost. This gift entitles a person to have the companionship of the Spirit anytime he or she is worthy of it and seeks it. More light! More truth! Thus, part of the good news is that we don't have to wander in the dark and stumble along the enmity–amity path. Instead, our Savior sheds forth light to clearly illuminate the way so that we can travel safely and confidently back to God.

# Children of God

*The Spirit itself beareth witness with
our spirit, that we are the children of God.*

Romans 8:16

**At times many of us let that enemy of achievement—
even the culprit 'self-defeat'—dwarf our aspirations,
smother our dreams, cloud our vision, and impair our
lives. The enemy's voice whispers in our ears, 'You
can't do it.' 'You're too young.' 'You're too old.' 'You're
nobody.' This is when we remember that we are created
in the image of God. Reflection on this truth provides a
profound sense of strength and power.**

Thomas S. Monson, "Choose You This Day," *Ensign*, Nov. 2004, 68

Children of a king and queen are princes and princesses.
Everyone knows that. We also know that princes and
princesses belong in the palace with the king and queen. Royal
children don't belong in the pigsty rolling around in the muck with
the pigs. Because of their status at birth, princes and princesses
are entitled to certain privileges. They are also entitled to certain
inheritances, all simply because of who their parents are.

While you and I may not be sons or daughters of an earthly
king, we are all spirit children of a heavenly king, God the Father.
Think about what that means. As a son or daughter of God, we
have inherited certain spiritual characteristics and privileges and
are heirs to an incredible legacy. While it is true that we were

born into a fallen, telestial world and have taken on a telestial, mortal body, our spirits are the offspring of a holy God, and thus our spirits are "genetically" holy.

If we truly understand that we are God's spirit children, we think of ourselves differently. Holiness is our genetic inheritance. How more royal could you be than to be God's own child? While sin can separate us from the holiness that is us, through repentance, baptism, the sacrament, and the grace of our Savior we can be restored to holiness. Because of Jesus Christ we can maintain our holiness even while journeying through a very unholy world.

However, if we don't understand our holy inheritance—if instead we think of ourselves as mortal, unholy beings faced with the task of becoming holy—we live life very differently. For example, if you have a new white jacket that you really like and you want to keep it new-looking and white, you act differently when wearing it than if you were wearing a dirty, old denim jacket that you care nothing about. In the beautiful white jacket, you avoid anything that would stain it. You try not to lie around in it because you don't want it to get wrinkled. You avoid activities that might rip or in any other way damage it, and if something happens to mar it, you quickly mend or clean it.

But in the old jacket, you might take a nap without even thinking about what will happen to the jacket. Or you might not only work in the jacket, but wipe your dirty hands on it. You don't care if you are playfully wrestling with friends and it gets ripped. You may even enjoy tearing it more just for a good laugh. You may think things like, "It's just an old jacket, so why bother? I'll get a new jacket next week, but for now I'll just do what I'm doing. It isn't that big of a deal."

Your attitude concerning the jacket determines how you treat it. And how you think about yourself determines how you act. If we think of ourselves as mortals trying to become holy, we often procrastinate the task. "I know I shouldn't be watching this movie, but one more time won't make a difference. I'll work on becoming holy next week." Or we think, "There's no way I can become holy. It's too difficult a task. There's too much to do. I just can't do it."

But if we acknowledge ourselves as holy beings, as children of God, as Latter-day *Saints*, we instinctively avoid anything that would contaminate us. We know we belong in the palace and not in the pigsty, and the smell of the sty is repulsive. We recognize the spark of divinity within us and refuse to go near anything that would douse that spark. We understand that we should spend our time learning how to care for the palace because it will someday be ours. Because we feel different, we act differently.

It is always easier to maintain a condition than it is to upgrade one. When we really feel that we are children of God, we innately resist anything that will take us away from Him. As Elder M. Russell Ballard said, "The most important, life-changing information that I know of is the knowledge that we are truly children of God our Eternal Father. This is not only doctrinally correct, it is spiritually vital" (M. Russell Ballard, "Like a Flame Unquenchable," *Ensign*, May 1999, 85). Knowing that we were born holy is vital. And through the Atonement of Jesus Christ, we can maintain that state of holiness by avoiding unholy things and by repenting when we slip from holiness.

The verses in Romans following the one that heads this chapter go on to say that the suffering of this present life can't be compared to the glory of what God has in store for us—the inheritance that is ours because we are the sons and daughters of the King. Mortals who understand their innate holiness are subject to vanity and other evils of mortality, but they will be delivered from "the bondage of corruption into the glorious liberty of the children of God" (Rom. 8:21).

As we conceive of ourselves as holy beings maintaining our holiness, the liberty and happiness promised us becomes easier to attain. Our own hearts proclaim the truth of it. Listen as the Spirit bears witness that you are a child of God and that as a spirit child of God you belong in His heavenly palace.

# Agents

*It is given unto them to know good from evil; wherefore
they are agents unto themselves, and I have given unto
you another law and commandment.*

Moses 6:56

**As the Lord's agents, we are bound by his law to do
what he wants us to do regardless of personal feelings
or worldly enticements.**

Joseph Fielding Smith, "Our Responsibilities as Priesthood Holders,"
*Ensign,* June 1971, 49

Many years ago, my husband and I left our children in
the care of some wonderful friends, the Buberts, while
we traveled to the Holy Land. While we were gone, our son
Joshua broke his leg and was taken to the hospital. Before we
left we had signed papers giving the Buberts legal authority to
act as agents for us in case of emergency. Therefore, when the
accident happened they were able to obtain the proper medical
attention for Josh as if they were his parents.

In the modern world, having agents that act in our behalf
is very common. We have insurance agents that take care of
our homes and cars whenever they are damaged. Real estate
agents look out for our best interest when we sell or buy a home.
Actors, writers, athletes, and others employ agents that promote
them and find them work. Consequently, we all know that a
good agent is one who protects and promotes what is best for

the person he or she represents.

These examples of modern-day agents also make it clear that the essence of being an agent is to do something for someone else. The dictionary tells us that an agent is someone who acts or exerts power or one who is authorized to act for or in the place of another. What we don't stop to think about often enough is that there are two parts to being an agent. First, as this definition makes clear, an agent has power to act for someone else, but inherent in this definition is the fact that the boundaries of a person's agency are limited.

The scriptures talk about the fact that God's children are "agents unto themselves" (D&C 29:39; D&C 58:28; D&C 104:17; Moses 6:56). While this phrase does mean that we have the power to act, we sometimes interpret it too narrowly. We read "unto" but think "for." It doesn't say in the verse that we are agents *for* ourselves. Instead we are agents *unto* ourselves.

The word *unto* isn't used much anymore; instead, it has been shortened to the simple preposition *to.* But it still means the same thing. While there are many ways *to* is used, the one that fits best in this context is that *to* is often followed by a word or phrase expressing a limit in extent, amount, or degree. The phrase "agents unto themselves" means that our moral agency is limited to ourselves. Our moral agency does not extend to our friends, or our spouses, or even our children. Our agency is limited unto ourselves. This could be compared to my insurance agent. She is an agent for me (acting in my behalf), but the boundaries of that agency are limited to the insurance company she is employed by—to the rules, regulations, and contract I have signed.

The phrase "agents unto themselves" makes clear that our moral agency is limited, but we still need to understand for whom we act as agents. Moses 6:56 explains that it is because we know good from evil that we are agents. And knowing good from evil, we are equipped to know God's will. Therefore, we can act for Heavenly Father and Jesus Christ, whose earth this is and who created all that is good. In other words, it is intended that we be agents for Jesus Christ. And as His agents we are charged with the task of protecting and promoting all that is good—all that is His. We are to act on behalf of Jesus Christ. As the angel taught Adam, "Thou shalt do all that thou doest in the name of the Son" (Moses 5:8). This means that at some point, we will be required to explain how we promoted and protected His good.

However, not everyone chooses to be an agent for Jesus Christ. Just as my insurance agent chooses which company she will represent, we choose whom we will represent— God or Satan. Recognizing that every time I make a choice between good and evil, I am acting as an agent to promote and encourage and influence one or the other, helps me to make correct choices.

God has trusted me and you to be His agents—to promote, advance, and encourage all that is good—all that is His. What an honor that is.

# The Law of Justice

*Prepare your souls for that glorious day*
*when justice shall be administered unto the righteous.*

2 Nephi 9:46

**God's mercy is the only source of the ultimate and eternal joy, which restores every loss, dries every tear, and erases every pain. Eternal joy transcends all suffering. In this life and in the life to come, that joy comes about through the Resurrection and the remission of sins.**

Dallin H. Oaks, "Joy and Mercy," *Ensign*, Nov. 1991, 73

It is highly likely that when we considered the topic of agency in the premortal life, we also discussed the matter of fairness. The reason I believe that the two topics were discussed together then is because they are discussed together now. Discussions, debates, books, and movies abound in which the question, Why do bad things happen to good people? is explored. The "why" of that question is answered in many ways, but the solution to the dilemma the question poses is found in the law of justice.

Elder Bruce R. McConkie explained  that *"justice demands that a penalty be paid for every violation of the Lord's laws"* (Bruce R. McConkie, *Mormon Doctrine* [Salt Lake City: Bookcraft, 1966], 406; emphasis in original). This is a true statement and is the way we usually think about and discuss the law of justice. When we sin, a penalty needs to be paid, and if we repent the Savior mercifully pays the penalty for us. But the scripture we began with says that we should prepare for the day when justice will be administered to the *righteous*. If justice is all about payment for sin, what does it have to do with the righteous?

A little thought brings us to the realization that paying the penalty for sin is only one side of the coin of justice. The other side represents the fact that if we have been sinned against or made to suffer through no fault of our own, justice demands that in some way we must be compensated. The Prophet Joseph Smith explained the importance of understanding this principle. He said that you can't have faith without understanding that God is absolutely just. After all, how can you have faith in a God that cannot make everything fair? As the Prophet goes on to explain, without an understanding of justice we could not place our confidence in Jesus Christ, but with an understanding of the justice of God there is "no room for doubt to get into the heart, and the mind is enabled to cast itself upon the Almighty without fear and without doubt, and with the most unshaken confidence, believing that the judge of all the earth will do right" (Joseph Smith, *Lectures on Faith: Delivered to the School of the Prophets in Kirtland, Ohio, 1834–35* [Salt Lake City: Deseret Book Co., 1835], 4:13).

A metaphor of automobiles helps me understand this. It is as if we are all cars—some of us Cadillac Sevilles, some Ford trucks, some Honda Civics, some BMW X5s, and some Hummers or Volkswagons. We are all different but in the beginning we are all formed and running perfectly for our mission in life. Then we are plopped down on the highway of life, and the very plopping damages some of us. We arrive with parts missing or not working properly. Others start down the highway just fine only to encounter engine problems. Some of us are parked and minding our own business when a thief damages or destroys us. Our beautiful paint job gets marred by storms, accidentally nicked by cars parked too close, and sometimes we are intentionally keyed or have a window smashed. Upholstery wears out or gets stained. Minor and major accidents damage the body of the car. Engine problems occur. Tires go bald or blow out. Brakes need replacing. In short, no car makes it down the highway without some damage, just as no human being makes it through life without damage. But the promise from the Savior is that every bit of damage we were not responsible for causing will be repaired and recompensed (justice). And if we repent and turn to Jesus Christ, every bit of damage we caused ourselves and others will also be fixed (mercy). The two principles work hand in hand to save us.

This is why Paul could say to the Romans, "All things work together for good to them that love God" (Rom. 8:28), and why the Lord could say to Joseph Smith in the midst of all his afflictions, "Search diligently, Pray always, and be believing, and all things shall work together for your good" (D&C 90:24). Elder Neal A. Maxwell declared, "The justice and mercy of God will have been so demonstrably perfect that at the Final Judgment there will be no complaints, including from those who once questioned what God had allotted in the mortal framework" (Neal A. Maxwell, "Content with the Things Allotted unto Us," *Ensign*, May 2000, 72). Because of the justice of God, all things will be made fair. Even the bad things can be made to work for our good. We will be healed and recompensed for every unfair hurt.

I once had a very dear friend who had gone blind. She

often said to me, "I hate being blind, but I would not trade the things I have learned from being blind for anything." She recognized that part of the recompense to her for being blind was the knowledge she had gained. In addition, she trusted that there were other compensations that she had not recognized or possibly yet received. She knew that because God is just, He would make everything absolutely fair.

# The Gift of the Holy Ghost

*Thus the Gospel began to be preached, from
the beginning, being declared by holy angels sent forth
from the presence of God, and by his own voice,
and by the gift of the Holy Ghost.*

Moses 5:58

**The gift of the Holy Ghost . . . quickens all the intellectual
faculties, increases, enlarges, expands and purifies all
the natural passions and affections; and adapts them,
by the gift of wisdom, to their lawful use. It inspires,
develops, cultivates and matures all the fine-toned
sympathies, joys, tastes, kindred feelings, and affections
of our nature. It inspires virtue, kindness, goodness,
tenderness, gentleness, and charity. It develops beauty
of person, form and features. It tends to health,
vigor, animation, and social feeling. It invigorates all
the faculties of the physical and intellectual man. It
strengthens, and gives tone to the nerves. In short, it is,
as it were, marrow to the bone, joy to the heart, light to
the eyes, music to the ears, and life to the whole being.**

Parley P. Pratt, *Key to the Science of Theology*, 9th ed.
(Salt Lake City: Deseret Book Co., 1965), 101

---

Every person born into the world is given the gift of light—
the Spirit of Christ (see Moroni 7:16). Because of this,
all people have a conscience or internal "homing device" that

can guide them back to God if they will listen to the feelings and promptings that come into their hearts. This is a marvelous gift. As Elder Robert D. Hales stated, "Light and darkness cannot occupy the same space at the same time. Where the light of Christ is found, the darkness of Lucifer, even Satan, must depart, defeated" (Robert D. Hales, "In Remembrance of Jesus," *Ensign,* Nov. 1997, 24). Therefore, as we cultivate this light, we expel darkness from our lives.

The Bible Dictionary tells us that the Light of Christ is "just what the words imply: enlightenment, knowledge, and an uplifting, ennobling, persevering influence that comes upon mankind because of Jesus Christ. For instance, Christ is 'the true light that lighteth every man that cometh into the world' (D&C 93:2; John 1:9)" (Bible Dictionary, "Light of Christ," 725).

Those who ignore the light of Christ they are born with sink to a level of animal instinct. Instead of following their hearts, these people follow the passions, lusts, and desires of the flesh. They are driven by appetites and greed. Like animals they act on physical instinct rather than on light and truth.

However, all who follow the promptings of the Light of Christ will eventually (whether in this life or the next) be led to the gospel of Jesus Christ, where they can obtain the gift of the Holy Ghost and gain more light and truth. This marvelous gift is "the right to have, whenever one is worthy, the companionship of the Holy Ghost. More powerful than that which is available before baptism, it acts as a cleansing agent to purify a person and sanctify him from all sin. Thus it is often spoken of as 'fire' (Matt. 3:11; 2 Ne. 31:17; D&C 19:31)" (Bible Dictionary, "Holy Ghost," 704).

When we are confirmed a member of the Church, we are

told to "receive the Holy Ghost." We are not informed that we will now have the Holy Ghost as a constant companion. What we are given is the "gift" of the Holy Ghost, and as the Bible Dictionary makes clear, the gift of the Holy Ghost is the *right* to have the Holy Ghost as a companion. But we must be worthy of that companionship, and we must seek it.

The following analogy helps me understand this. If someone gives me a beautiful decorative telephone, I could set it on my table and admire how nice it looks there and even enjoy the beauty of the telephone. In that way I could consider it a wonderful gift, but there is so much more. The phone doesn't serve me as intended unless I activate it or plug it into the proper source. Once activated, if the phone rings and I refuse to pick up the receiver and listen, it doesn't help me at all. I don't receive the information intended for me. Or if I never lift the receiver and make a call to ask for help or information, of what use is the phone to me?

In this analogy, plugging into the source can be compared to being worthy and being connected to our source, Jesus Christ. Obviously, answering the phone is obeying the promptings we receive, and making a call is communing with our Father in Heaven through prayer. Thus, the phone is like the gift of the Holy Ghost. Being in contact with the person on the other end of the line is like receiving the Holy Ghost. As we take advantage of the gift in these ways, the Holy Ghost is with us, and when He is with us He changes us. He sanctifies and cleanses us and makes us new creatures in Christ.

Too often we operate by the Light of Christ and think that is all there is. We don't realize that there is more out there. We don't take advantage of all that Christ offers us. Through repentance and by drawing close to the Holy Ghost, we gain power and more light. Therefore, as Sheri Dew suggested, we need to ask, "What are we willing to do, what weaknesses and indulgences will we give up, to have as our personal protector and guide the constant companionship of the Holy Ghost?" (Sheri Dew, "We Are Not Alone," *Ensign*, Nov. 1998, 94).

Whatever we need to do to enjoy the companionship of the Holy Ghost, it is worth it. The Holy Ghost not only guides but sanctifies and purifies us. This strengthens us to overcome the negative influences of telestial life. Among other things, it gives us the power to overcome despair, discouragement, and temptation. It gives us the power to nurture and help our loved ones and to serve in our callings and to fulfill all our other responsibilities in a righteous way.

All people born into the world have the light of Christ to guide them to the truth. But only those who have been given the gift of the Holy Ghost by the authority of the priesthood have the right to His constant companionship—and to the sanctifying power it brings. If we don't understand the difference between the light of Christ and the gift of the Holy Ghost, we may not realize that the gift of the Holy Ghost offers us so much more than guidance. As we pray for the Holy Ghost to be with us and then live worthy of and use that gift, we are changed and empowered to become like God.

# The Workings of the Holy Ghost

*And after they had been received unto baptism,
and were wrought upon and cleansed by the power of
the Holy Ghost, they were numbered among the
people of the church of Christ; and their names were
taken, that they might be remembered and nourished by
the good word of God, to keep them in the right
way, to keep them continually watchful unto prayer,
relying alone upon the merits of Christ, who was
the author and the finisher of their faith.*

Moroni 6:4

**Not having the gift of the Holy Ghost is somewhat like
having a body without an immune system.**

James E. Faust, "Born Again," *Ensign*, May 2001, 54

In the Church, we often hear stories of how the Spirit guides a person to do something that turns out to help someone else or that brings about other wonderful consequences. But the scriptures teach us that the Holy Ghost *works* on us, meaning that He often pushes us out of our comfort zone and sometimes even leads us to experiences that may be difficult.

Years ago, I met a man whose conversion story illustrates this point. Pat had been raised in the South by alcoholic parents who eventually died from the effects of alcoholism. The story began when Pat celebrated the birth of his second son by doing what his father had taught him to do: he went out and got drunk.

The next morning, hung over and feeling terrible, Pat went to the mirror to shave, but it was not his own face he saw reflected. It was his father's! Frightened, Pat spoke aloud, "I'm just like my dad!" And at that moment he committed to never drink another drop of alcohol again—a promise he kept.

Shortly after this experience, Pat was on a business trip when a man beside him on the airplane asked, "Excuse me, but are you a Mormon?" Irritated, Pat replied in colorful bar-room language that he was not.

A few months later while traveling to a seminar in Wisconsin, Pat caught the limousine service into town. A fellow passenger, the city manager in Juno, Alaska, was wearing a watch with gold nuggets attached to the band. Pat asked about the nuggets and the man told him he had panned the gold himself. After a few minutes of pleasant conversation the man asked Pat, "By any chance, are you a Mormon?" Pat let out a stream of expletives and ended the conversation with an emphatic, "No!"

A few months later in an airport in Detroit, Pat was looking up, examining the beautiful domed ceiling when someone tapped him on the shoulder and asked, "Excuse me, but are you a Mormon?" Again Pat swore at the man and told him, "No!"

A while later, Pat was in Texas in a taxi en route to the first day of a class to be taught by a scientist at NASA. As they approached NASA, one of Pat's business associates told him, "Pat, during these classes you are going to have to watch your language. This scientist is a religious man and he will ask you to leave if you talk the way you usually do." This irritated Pat, but he needed the information and so he grudgingly held his tongue as he sat through the classes.

A week later, his business partners needed some papers from the scientist, and Pat was the only person available to pick them up. Reluctantly, Pat agreed to go. When Pat arrived at the office, the secretary had the papers he needed, so Pat retrieved them and left, relieved that he wouldn't have to talk with the "stuffy" man. But he only got a few steps down the hall when he heard someone call his name. He turned to see the scientist. They exchanged a few cordial words and then the scientist said, "I watched you during our sessions and couldn't help wondering, are you a Mormon?"

By now Pat had grown very curious. He had no idea what a Mormon was, and since he couldn't answer in his normal bar-room fashion, he simply asked, "What's going on?"

For the next few hours while touring NASA, the scientist told Pat about the Church. Pat was impressed, so when he returned home, he looked in the yellow pages of his phone book for a Mormon Church, but could find nothing. For the next few weeks he asked everyone he encountered if they had heard of the Mormon Church. No one had. Finally, someone answered him by saying, "Yes, I think the real name is the Church of Jesus Christ of Latter-day Saints." With that information, Pat went back to the phone book and found an LDS meetinghouse not far from his home, and he attended a meeting there the following Sunday. Liking what he heard, he returned the next week. This was before the three-hour meeting block, and he happened to attend priesthood meeting, leaving as soon as the closing prayer was said.

After Pat attended priesthood meeting for a few weeks, something unusual began to happen. Pat repeatedly awoke in the middle of the night with a feeling he couldn't understand.

The strange feeling would cause him to weep. He'd sneak out of bed and go to the living room, where he would cover his head with a pillow so his wife wouldn't hear him. Once "hidden," he would cry uncontrollably. This caused him to worry that he was having a nervous breakdown.

Then, after priesthood meeting one Sunday, Pat was looking for a rest room and opened a door to what he later learned was a Junior Sunday School room. But before he could shut the door the woman conducting the meeting said, "Oh, children, look, we have a stake visitor with us!" As the woman promptly ushered Pat to the front of the room and sat him down, he thought, "Why does this woman think I look like a side of meat?" He was so confused that he didn't even try to protest.

When he finally was able to collect his thoughts, the meeting had resumed, so he stayed. That day the children were having a testimony meeting. He listened as one by one they came forward and bore simple testimonies of the Church, the Savior, and modern prophets. As they did, the feeling that had awakened him during the nights began to seep through him and the tears began to come. But this time he recognized it as the Spirit of God.

The next Sunday, Pat asked to see the pastor and someone pointed him in the direction of the bishop. Pat asked the man if he could join the Church, and the bishop introduced him to two young men standing nearby who wore dark suits and name tags. The next Saturday, June 5, 1975, Pat was baptized a member of the Church—two years after his experience with the mirror.

While many people played important parts in Pat's conversion, the only one who knows he did is the scientist from NASA. But Pat is the first to acknowledge that the three men who previously asked him if he was a Mormon played important parts as well. They prepared him to listen.

The question you and I should ask ourselves is what our reaction would be if we followed a prompting to ask someone, "Are you a Mormon?" and they cursed and swore at us like Pat did. Would we walk away thinking, "That's the last time I do that?" or, "That couldn't have possibly been the Spirit?" Or would we say, "I don't understand what just happened, but I trust that the Lord does"?

More importantly, the next time we felt the prompting to do something, would we think, "I'm not going there again! I remember what happened last time"? Or would we simply do what we were prompted to do, trusting that "God moves in a mysterious way, His wonders to perform" ("God Moves in a Mysterious Way," *Hymns,* no. 48)?

# That Which Edifies

*That which doth not edify is not of God,*
*and is darkness. That which is of God is light;*
*and he that receiveth light, and continueth in*
*God, receiveth more light; and that light groweth*
*brighter and brighter until the perfect day.*

Doctrine and Covenants 50:23–24

**I do not want my mind to be a dumping place for shabby ideas or thoughts, for disappointments, bitterness, envy, shame, hatred, worry, grief, or jealousy. If you are fretting over such things, it's time to clean the yard. Get rid of all that junk! Get rid of it! Put up a No Trespassing sign, a No Dumping sign, and take control of yourself. Don't keep anything that will not edify you.**

Boyd K. Packer, *That All May Be Edified* (Salt Lake City: Deseret Book Co., 1982), 65

---

Today the word *edify* means to uplift or enlighten or encourage. It is a word we hear often in Church talks and lessons. But when I came to understand the history or etymology of the word, *edify* took on new significance. *Edify* comes into the English language from the Latin words *aedes,* which means "temple," and *ficare,* which means "to make." Thus, *edify* originally meant "to make or erect a temple." And what is a temple? The *Oxford English Dictionary* describes it as "an edifice devoted to divine worship," and "any place regarded as occupied by the divine presence."

When we consider that the scriptures declare the body to be a temple, this is especially instructive. Jesus compared His body to a temple (see John 2:21). His body was a temple because a divine presence resided within it.

Paul chastised the people of Corinth by saying: "Know ye not that ye are the temple of God, and that the Spirit of God dwelleth in you? If any man defile the temple of God, him shall God destroy; for the temple of God is holy, which temple ye are" (1 Cor. 3:16–17). Later, Paul asked, "What? know ye not that your body is the temple of the Holy Ghost which is in you, which ye have of God, and ye are not your own?" (1 Cor. 6:19).

From these scriptures we learn that our bodies are intended to be the dwelling place of the Holy Ghost, the third member of the Godhead. Our bodies are meant to be a holy habitation. They were created for the purpose of being edified.

Understanding this helps us establish a criteria for what is edifying and what is not. If something contributes to creating a place where the Holy Ghost can dwell, it is edifying. If something does not contribute to a place where the Holy Ghost can dwell, it is not edifying. Sterling W. Sill declared, "One of our most urgent present-day needs is to houseclean our thinking. Because two opposite thoughts cannot co-exist in the mind at the same moment, the best way to get rid of undesirable thoughts is by antedoting them with good. The best way to get darkness out of a room is to fill it with light. The best way to kill the negative is to cultivate the positive, and the best way to improve our lives is to improve our thoughts" (Sterling W. Sill, *Conference Report,* Oct. 1959, 103).

But how can we improve our thoughts? How can we choose only that which edifies when there are so very many factors that come to bear upon us each day?

Much research has been done lately by psychologists who are surprised by the way people can be prejudiced by subtle influences in their environment. For example, one experiment measured the speed and gait of people coming into an office to take a simple test. The test consisted of 10 scrambled-word sentences. The participants were to unscramble the words to make complete sentences as quickly as possible. The sentences, however, all contained words that made one think of old age. The participants were then observed as they left the test, and almost all moved slower and in a more labored fashion. The researchers concluded that when the idea of old age was planted in the participants' minds, they subconsciously thought older and thus moved slower.

In another experiment, two groups of people were given scrambled words from which they had to create sentences. In one group, the words planted ideas of aggressive behavior, and in the other group the words suggested passive behavior. After the participants unscrambled the words, they were ushered into the office of a psychologist who purposely ignored them and made them wait for him to finish what he was doing. The group with the aggressive words became agitated and hostile. The group with the passive words waited patiently. (See Malcolm Gladwell, *Blink* [New York: Little, Brown and Co., 2005], 52–55.)

Most of these researchers use their findings to support the idea that as mortal beings we are programmed to think and do certain things. This can happen; however, the scriptures teach us that we have a choice as to what we do and how we react. If we consciously consider what we are doing, we can control the thoughts and feelings that direct our lives. King Benjamin tells us, "If ye do not watch yourselves, and your thoughts, and your words, and your deeds, and observe the commandments of God, and continue in the faith of what ye have heard concerning the coming of our Lord, even unto the end of your lives, ye must perish" (Mosiah 4:30).

While we don't always have control of whether a thought bursts into our heads or not, we certainly have control over whether we savor it or cast it out. One important thing to realize is that there is more than one way to "savor" or continue to think a bad thought. It is obvious that if we dwell on the thought in a covetous or desirous way, we are savoring it and refusing to cast it aside. But we also cling to a thought when we tell ourselves, "Oh, I shouldn't have thought that. I'm such a bad person. I let this thought get into my head. I am so terrible. I think bad thoughts! This thought keeps coming into my head. I am so terrible." Either way of thinking is a way of dwelling on the bad thought. What we need to do is recognize that in a telestial world we are going to occasionally have bad thoughts thrust upon us. Our job is to push them out of our minds by replacing them with something good.

When we recognize the power of suggestion and subconscious thinking, we also realize how important it is to create as much good as possible in the controllable facets of our environment. As Elder Russell M. Nelson said, "We are to honor the body as a temple of God, and allow no forbidden thought, sight, sound, or substance to enter its sacred precincts" (Russell M. Nelson, *The Gateway We Call Death* [Salt Lake City: Deseret Book Co., 1995], 6).

To follow this apostolic counsel, we need to edify ourselves.

We do this by surrounding ourselves with colors, pictures, music, sayings, and decor that lift and encourage. We can train ourselves to be more aware of how things affect us, and to be discriminating as to what we do for entertainment. Although in a telestial world we will never be able to avoid all negative, unholy things, we can learn how best to let only that which edifies into our lives. We can be more aware that we are a temple for the Holy Ghost, and we can seek more actively to find and incorporate that which edifies into our lives.

# It's All in the Perspective

*For now we see through a glass, darkly;*

*but then face to face: now I know in part; but*

*then shall I know even as also I am known.*

1 Corinthians 13:12

**Look at everything through the lens of eternity. If you will do this, life will take on a different perspective.**

James E. Faust, "Instruments in the Hands of God," *Ensign*, Nov. 2005, 114

There are some moments in life that change you forever. One of those happened to me many years ago during a Relief Society lesson. I don't remember what the lesson was about, but somehow it had turned into a discussion of husbands' faults. One after another of the sisters began to complain about her husband's lack of responsiveness or his failure to help out around the house, etc. You've all been in a situation like that and know how contagious negative feelings are.

At the time, my husband was bishop and our ward was very large. He was gone almost every night, leaving me to care for our five children under the age of eight. In short, I felt overwhelmed and alone, so as I listened to the other women complain, my husband's faults and failings kept popping into my head. With every new comment from the group, another fault of his would come to mind and I'd think, "Yea, my husband does that too!" or "That isn't half as bad as what Carl does (or doesn't) do!"

The Relief Society instructor failed to get the class back

on track, and as the comments got more negative so did the feelings within me. I didn't vocalize them, but I certainly was thinking them, and those thoughts were generating all kinds of hot, negative feelings within me.

But then something happened that changed me. A woman in the back of the room began to rave about how her husband made a mess in the entryway every time he came home from work. He worked construction and he'd take off his dirty boots as soon as he entered the house, drop them near the door, walk into the family room, plop down to watch the evening news, and pull off his stinky socks, dropping them beside the couch for her to pick up later. "It's disgusting," she said, and several women nodded in agreement.

But at that point the elderly woman sitting in front of me, who had been a widow for 23 years, turned to her gray-haired friend sitting next to her, a widow of 19 years, and whispered, "I wish I had socks on my floor."

I'm sure that besides the friend, I am the only person in the room that heard those words—words that pierced my heart and instantly erased all my negative thoughts and feelings. In that moment, my perspective shifted from that of victim of my husband's thoughtlessness to that of grateful wife. I had someone to pick up after—what a blessing!

That day the words "I wish I had socks on my floor" sunk deep into my soul, never to be forgotten. They come to mind often, especially when I am tempted to re-catalog my husband's faults. And I learned that perspective is everything.

In the realm of spiritual things, these kinds of shifts in thinking are what life is all about. As we learn and grow in gospel precepts, the Spirit whispers the exact thing we need to hear at the exact moment we need to hear it. Line upon line, precept upon precept, we then change our attitudes and become new creatures. The negative, carnal, and sensual is burned from us, and as we become pure and holy, we see life differently. Our perspective of who we are, who others are, what situations mean in our life—and a myriad of other things—changes.

An ant perceives a hill to be a very different thing than what a bird perceives it to be. As children of God, however, our view is not determined by altitude but by attitude. We realize that perspective changes depending upon the mental position we see things from, and we more fully appreciate the fact that a loving Heavenly Father not only has a better perspective, but a perfect perspective. Elder Russell M. Nelson declared, "I know that an all-wise Heavenly Father's perspective is much broader than is ours. While we know of our mortal problems and pain, He knows of our immortal progress and potential. If we pray to know His will and submit ourselves to it with patience and courage, heavenly healing can take place in His own way and time" (Russell M. Nelson, "Jesus Christ—the Master Healer," *Ensign*, Nov. 2005, 85).

Analyzing and being open minded about our own perspective is *life changing*, and fully recognizing that God's perspective is perfect is *healing*. Both help us to let go of worries and concerns and to trust more fully in Him.

# Gratitude

*And he who receiveth all things with thankfulness shall*
*be made glorious; and the things of this earth shall be*
*added unto him, even an hundred fold, yea, more.*

Doctrine and Covenants 78:19

**When we give thanks in all things, we see hardships and adversities in the context of the purpose of life. We are sent here to be tested. There must be opposition in all things. We are meant to learn and grow through that opposition, through meeting our challenges, and through teaching others to do the same.**

Dallin H. Oaks, "Give Thanks in All Things," *Ensign*, May 2003, 95

When my children were growing up, I loved telling them the story of Daniel in the lion's den. I usually taught it in the context of prayer and pointed out how Daniel prayer even when he knew that the penalty for praying was to be thrown into a den of lions, "He went into his house; and his windows being open in his chamber toward Jerusalem, he kneeled upon his knees three times a day, and prayed" (Daniel 6:10). The story impressed my children, and every time I told the story I felt the awe and amazement again. Such faith, such devotion to God! Prayer was so important to Daniel that he continued to pray even when he knew he might be put to death for doing so.

Recently, I reread this story and felt the old surge of awe, but this time I noticed something new. The verse I just quoted goes on to say that Daniel "gave thanks before his God, as he did aforetime." Daniel had been taken captive while a young man and hauled into a foreign country. Who knows what dreams or ambitions were thwarted by that captivity? Who knows what abuse he suffered at the hands of his captors? Who knows how many friends and loved ones were killed or left behind, never to be seen again? And he was grateful?

Once in Babylon, Daniel was given privileges and treated well by the king, but after years of training he was being persecuted by his peers. They plotted to kill him because of their jealousy. Yet Daniel did not pray to be freed from the persecution of the men who sought so diligently to destroy him. He didn't complain to God about the horrible path his life had taken or the awful situation he was in. Despite the persecution and adversity, despite the threat to his life, Daniel prayed to thank the Lord—*just as he had always done before!*

In the Doctrine and Covenants the Lord says, "Thou shalt thank the Lord thy God in all things" (59:7). He doesn't say that we are to thank Him for all good things or to thank Him whenever things go the way we want them to go. Instead, we are to thank the Lord in *all* things, which to me means all good or even what we consider bad things. But how do we do that? How do we bring ourselves to the point that we can give thanks for the rotten days, and the bad breaks, and the unfulfilled dreams, and the persecution from others? Do we put our head in the sand and pretend everything is wonderful? I don't think so.

The secret to answering these questions may be found in a synonym of the word *thankful*—the word *grateful*. The *Oxford English Dictionary* defines *grateful* as "pleasing to the mind or the senses, agreeable, acceptable, welcome." That definition seems to imply that we can only be grateful for what is pleasant and nice, and leaves us still wondering about the not-so-wonderful. But the words *grateful* and *grace* both come from the same Latin root, *gratus*. Grace is one of the defining characteristics of God. Grace is unmerited love, favor, enabling power, mercy, assistance, and much more. Grace is what God gives us. And because He gives so much now and will give even more in the future, we can be grateful that He will make all things perfect, fair, and right.

In the bad times, we can be grateful for God's grace that enables us to endure. We can be grateful for His grace that tempers even the bad so that it is not more than we can endure. We can be grateful for His grace that turns even the difficult situations into learning and growing experiences that make us more like Him. We can give thanks in all things because of God's goodness. We can give thanks that even in our darkest hours His light is with us. All we need to do is open our hearts and let it in.

# Good Works

*By their works ye shall know them; for if their*
*works be good, then they are good also.*

Moroni 7:4–5

**The sacred scriptures provide for you and me a model to follow when they declare, "Jesus increased in wisdom and stature, and in favour with God and man" (Luke 2:52). And He "went about doing good, . . . for God was with him" (Acts 10:38).**

Thomas S. Monson, "Anxiously Engaged," *Ensign*, Nov. 2004, 56

As Mormon begins his great teachings on faith, hope, and charity, he explains that he is speaking to the "peaceable followers of Christ" and that he knows the people are peaceable followers of Christ because he has seen their works. In other words, Mormon knows them by their actions. The hope for me is in the fact that he doesn't recognize them as followers of Christ because they are perfect or without flaw. Instead, he acknowledges them as followers of Christ because they try to do good.

What follows in Moroni 7 is a qualification of what it means to do good. Mormon explains that good isn't determined by the act itself but rather by the intent that motivates the act. For example, many people go to church because they love God and want to worship Him. At that moment, they would rather be in church worshipping and partaking of the sacrament than be anywhere else in the world. Other people attend church meetings for selfish reasons. Perhaps a man sells cars and wants to create an image of himself as a good church-going person so that everyone will trust him and buy cars from him. His action—going to church—is correct, but his motivation is wrong. Therefore, without "real intent it profiteth him nothing" (Moroni 7:6).

So if our motives aren't absolutely pure and perfect, should we stay home from church? No! The reason we go to church is to be changed. We go hoping that the good there will "rub off" on us, hoping our hearts will be touched, hoping we will be taught how to love to worship, hoping our motives will be made pure. The key is to realize that our hearts need to change— that we need to be part of the good not just look like the good, President Monson explained, "Our task is to become our best selves. One of God's greatest gifts to us is the joy of trying again, for no failure ever need be final" (Thomas S. Monson, "The Will Within," *Ensign*, May 1987, 67). This trying again isn't just about the action, but it is also about trying again until, instead of obeying grudgingly, our heart rejoices in obedience.

As the scriptures admonish, "Men should be anxiously engaged in a good cause, and do many things of their own free will, and bring to pass much righteousness; For the power is in them, wherein they are agents unto themselves. And inasmuch as men do good they shall in nowise lose their reward" (D&C 58:21–28).

This brings up another problem concerning good. Notice that the verse doesn't say we have to do *all* good. We only have to do good. Often the good that needs to be done in any given moment is defined for us, like feeding a hungry infant when it cries, or nurturing a child or friend when he or she is hurt, or going to church on Sunday. On other occasions, our time is more discretionary and we must choose between options that are good—like visiting a sick neighbor, taking the family on an outing, studying our scriptures, or going to the temple. Sometimes the Spirit will tell us which of these we should choose to do, but more often it is left entirely up to us. At these times Elder Oaks has admonished us to choose not just the good, but the best. He said, "Some things are better than good, and these are the things that should command priority attention in our lives" (Dallin H. Oaks, "Good, Better, Best," *Ensign*, Nov. 2007, 104).

But even when we have taken a stand and are choosing the best things to do with our time, the adversary doesn't leave us alone. He just changes his tactics, and he works all the harder to bring us down. He still wants to derail us, and if he finds he can't tempt us with evil, he'll tempt us with discouragement. As soon as we have made our choice for good, he begins to taunt us about all the other good things we didn't choose to do. As Elder Oaks continued, "The number of good things we can do far exceeds the time available to accomplish them" (ibid).

As the adversary points these other things out, we begin to spiritually beat ourselves up because we didn't do all of the other good things we "should" have done. But nowhere in scripture are we commanded to do all good simultaneously—every possible good act—or even all good in a lifetime! That is impossible. We can't feed the baby, exercise our body, earn money, cook dinner, write to missionaries, do family history work, attend the temple, prepare our Sunday lesson, help the neighbors move, do our home and visiting teaching, attend to the needy, and study our scriptures all in the same moment. Just try to picture someone doing all that; it isn't even imaginable! We live in a sequential time sphere. And that makes tasks sequential. Even trying to accomplish all of these things in one day is absurd. And yet we often go to bed at night feeling inadequate because we haven't done it all.

God knows that the world He created is a linear, time-bound world, and that we can only do one thing at a time. He doesn't expect more. But He also wants us to know, as Elder Joseph B. Wirthlin said, that "we can fill our lives with good, leaving no room for anything else. We have so much good from which to choose that we need never partake of evil" (Joseph B. Wirthlin, "Seeking the Good," *Ensign,* May 1992, 86).

God's promise is that blessings will come to us if what we do is good. So do good—all the good that you enjoy doing in the moment that is appropriate for that good thing—and then bask in the marvelous feeling that comes from doing good. That is joy.

God simply asks that in any given moment we choose, from among the many options that confront us, the best good for that moment.

# Good Courage

*Be strong and of a good courage, fear not, nor be afraid*
*of them: for the Lord thy God, he it is that doth go*
*with thee; he will not fail thee, nor forsake thee.*

Deuteronomy 31:6

**Cultivate an attitude of happiness. Cultivate a spirit of optimism. Walk with faith, rejoicing in the beauties of nature, in the goodness of those you love, in the testimony which you carry in your heart concerning things divine.**

Gordon B. Hinckley, "If Thou Art Faithful," *Ensign*, Nov. 1984, 89

When Moses was translated, the task of leading the children of Israel into the promised land fell upon Joshua. This meant that Joshua would first need to clear the land of its present inhabitants and, while waging war, encourage his people to be faithful and righteous. With that daunting task ahead of him, Joshua was given the following charge: "Be thou strong and very courageous, that thou mayest observe to do according to all the law, which Moses my servant commanded thee: turn not from it to the right hand or to the left, that thou mayest prosper whithersoever thou goest. This book of the law shall not depart out of thy mouth; but thou shalt meditate therein day and night, that thou mayest observe to do according to all that is written therein: for then thou shalt make thy way prosperous, and then thou shalt have good success. Have not I commanded thee? Be strong and of a good courage; be not afraid, neither be thou dismayed: for the Lord thy God is with thee whithersoever thou goest" (Josh. 1:6–9).

Through the years, I have read and reread this charge, and over time I adopted the last verse, which begins, *Have not I commanded thee?*, as my own charge. Then one day as I read it, I was struck—as if I'd never read it before—by three things. First of all, at the beginning of the charge the Lord tells Joshua that it is a commandment to be of good courage, to not be afraid or dismayed. It wasn't just good advice or wisdom, but it was a commandment. The second thing that struck me was the term *good courage.* Why did the Lord find it necessary to modify the word *courage?* And why did He follow the command to have courage with the command to "not be afraid"? Wasn't that redundant? Something seemed to be going on here that I wasn't catching. To me *courage* meant *bravery,* and isn't all bravery good? I guess that point can be argued—people can be brave in doing evil and that would be bad—but that thought didn't seem to fit here.

It took a while, but I finally discovered that when translators worked on the King James version of the Old Testament, the word *courage* did not mean bravery. It meant "feelings or passions of the heart" (John Ayto, *Dictionary of Word Origins* [New York: Little, Brown and Co., 1990], 141). Feelings and passions include things like lust, anger, love, hate, and mercy. Suddenly the charge made sense to me. Joshua was being charged to let only good feelings and passions into his heart. He was to have only the best of feelings.

But that made the third thing that struck me even more relevant. In this world of murder and anger and terrorism and rape and pillage, how can we exist and at the same time keep out all the fear, terror, worry, anguish, hate, and the myriad of other negative feelings and passions of the heart that bombard us daily?

Should we stop reading the newspaper or listening to the news? Should we bury our heads in the sand and close our eyes to all that is going on around us? Should we deny all evil and pretend everything is rosy and wonderful? No, we shouldn't, and we can't. Instead, we learn to filter out the bad. We learn to acknowledge that bad exists but not let it weigh us down or entice us to be part of it. We cling to and savor only good. In that way we let only the best of feelings into our hearts. We refuse to fear. We push away discouragement and despair. While all the negative human elements such as worry, anxiety, stress, and fatigue will assail us, we can refuse to let them take up permanent residence in our hearts. And how in the world can we do that? The answer is part of Joshua's charge: by constantly remembering that the Lord our God is with us whithersoever we go.

# Peace on Earth

*And the angel said unto them, Fear not: for, behold, I
bring you good tidings of great joy, which shall be to
all people. For unto you is born this day in the city of
David a Saviour, which is Christ the Lord.*

Luke 2:10–11

**Those who have felt the touch of the Master's hand
somehow cannot explain the change which comes
into their lives. There is a desire to live better, to serve
faithfully, to walk humbly, and to be more like the Savior.
Having received their spiritual eyesight and glimpsed
the promises of eternity, they echo the words of the
blind man to whom Jesus restored sight: 'One thing I
know, that, whereas I was blind, now I see' (John 9:25).**

Thomas S. Monson, "Anxiously Engaged," 58

One of the greatest events in the history of the world was
the birth of Jesus Christ. For centuries, people awaited the
promised event that would overturn the devastating effects of
the Fall. Finally, the Son of God came to save all mankind from
eternal misery and everlasting damnation. In utter jubilation,
the heavens opened and good people heard angels rejoicing.
Mortal men and women who lived by the Spirit recognized the
baby as the promised Messiah and shouted for joy.

Simeon, upon seeing the baby in the temple cried out, "Mine

eyes have seen thy salvation, Which thou hast prepared before the face of all the people; A light to lighten the Gentiles, and the glory of thy people Israel" (Luke 2:30–32). When the prophetess Anna saw the baby, she raised her voice to thank God for the Messiah and began to spread the good news that the Prince of Peace was at last upon the earth.

But many others did not see anything unusual. To them, this was just a baby—a baby who made messes and cried like any other baby. A baby born in a lowly stable, of all places. A baby born to parents of no status and no apparent consequence.

Hundreds of years before the Birth, an incident foreshadowed these divergent attitudes. While wandering in the wilderness, the children of Israel were plagued by fiery serpents whose bite was fatal. When Moses prayed to know what to do, the Lord told him to make a pole topped with a brass serpent and to erect it in the camp of Israel. Moses obeyed and then instructed the people who were bitten to look to the brass pole. And as we read in Numbers 21:9, "If a serpent had bitten any man, when he beheld the serpent of brass, he lived." Nephi recounts this story and adds that "because of the simpleness of the way, or the easiness of it, there were many who perished" (1 Ne. 17:41).

The same brass serpent that brought great healing relief to those who believed, was a thing of naught to others who perished. The same Baby that caused jubilation in the hearts of shepherds, wise men, and prophets was dismissed as a thing of naught by others. Even worse, some, like Herod, saw the Child as a threat that needed to be eliminated. It was the greatest news in all the world, but they didn't recognize it. They couldn't understand. They didn't see.

Some things haven't changed much. Prophets still tell us to

look to Christ, and if our hearts are set upon that which is good, we can see God in the most ordinary circumstances. Then we are not only healed but eagerly raise our voices in joy and praise, "Unto us a child is born, unto us a son is given" (Isa. 9:6).

# The New Star

*And behold, there shall a new star arise,*
*such an one as ye never have beheld; and*
*this also shall be a sign unto you.*

Helaman 14:5

**All the faithful Saints, all of those who have endured to the end, depart this life with the absolute guarantee of eternal life. There is no equivocation, no doubt, no uncertainty in our minds. Those who have been true and faithful in this life will not fall by the wayside in the life to come. If they keep their covenants here and now and depart this life firm and true in the testimony of our blessed Lord, they shall come forth with an inheritance of eternal life.**

Bruce R. McConkie, "The Dead Who Die in the Lord," *Ensign*, Nov. 1976, 106

---

When the Savior was born, great signs occurred in the heavens. A bright, new star appeared. In the New World, the sun went down but darkness never came, and the sky remained as if it were noonday. In the Old World, an angel proclaimed the glad tidings to shepherds tending their flocks: "Suddenly there was with the angel a multitude of the heavenly host praising God, and saying, Glory to God in the highest, and on earth peace, good will to men" (Luke 2:14).

At the time of the Savior's death, there were also signs. This time in the New World, the sun was darkened, along with the moon and the stars. For hours the earth shook violently and the skies ripped with thunder and lightning. When the storm ended, the face of the earth had completely changed, and for three long days there was no light upon the land—not even the tiny flame of a candle.

I often ponder on the symbolism and messages in these happenings. As Alma declared after his miraculous conversion, "Marvel not that all mankind, yea, men and women, all nations, kindreds, tongues and people, must be born again; yea, born of God, changed from their carnal and fallen state, to a state of righteousness, being redeemed of God, becoming his sons and daughters" (Mosiah 27:25). Thus we learn that all of us must be born again—born of Christ and made new by Him.

Strikingly, the symbols of His earthly birth are also the symbols of our new birth. When we are born again, a new "star"—Jesus Christ—arises in us, and His light shines like noonday sun even when the darkest trials and temptations befall us. The Savior's light guides us through the dark experiences and back into the presence of God.

But if we refuse to follow Christ and instead dwell in sin, we experience spiritual death, which causes the light to go out. At first that darkness might not be apparent to us, but as we persist in wandering in sin and refusing to repent, we must eventually pay for our sins. As the Savior explained, "If they would not repent they must suffer even as I; Which suffering caused myself even God, the greatest of all, to tremble because of pain, and to bleed at every pore, and to suffer both body and spirit" (D&C 19:17–18). Indeed, at this point, if we have chosen not to follow Christ, we will suffer the very depths of hell.

It is easy to understand why the angels sang what the King

James translators recorded as "Glory to God in the highest, and on earth peace, good will to men" (Luke 2:14). A better translation of the original Greek is "Glory to God in the highest and on earth peace upon men of good will." That is what His birth is all about: to bring peace to those who use their will to do good—those who emulate Him, who accept Him, who fill their hearts with His light and His goodness. For those who refuse to accept Him, there is no peace.

But the call still rings out from the prophets of the Lord to all who will listen, "Come walk in the light and experience the peace that comes to men of good will."

# Faith

*[The Lord] doth require that ye should do*
*as he hath commanded you; for which if ye*
*do, he doth immediately bless you.*

Mosiah 2:24

**We're not going to survive in this world, temporally or spiritually, without increased faith in the Lord— and I don't mean a positive mental attitude—I mean downright solid faith in the Lord Jesus Christ. That is the one thing that gives vitality and power to otherwise rather weak individuals.**

A. Theodore Tuttle, "Developing Faith," *Ensign*, Nov. 1986, 72

---

In his last sermon, King Benjamin promised the people of Zarahemla that if they would do what the Lord commanded them, they would immediately be blessed. Benjamin's powerful words reached into the hearts of his people, causing them to examine their lives and repent. But this particular promise from that sermon bothered me for a number of years.

Growing up in the Church with parents who loved and obeyed the Lord, I often heard stories about the amazing blessings that came from living the commandments. In addition to my parents' teachings, one Primary teacher in particular drilled into our young heads that if we would keep the Word of Wisdom, we would "run and not be weary, and . . . walk and not faint" (D&C 89:20). She had a way of turning every lesson into a Word of Wisdom lesson and was fond of quoting this verse.

The problem was that I had a friend with rheumatoid arthritis who could not walk, let alone run. Sherida and I were the same age, and our fathers had been friends for years. Their group of friends got together several times a year, and one of my earliest memories is of one of those gatherings, a picnic at Liberty Park. My dad was pushing me on the swing, so high that I felt like I was flying—my toes reaching into the sky, my stomach rolling with the lift and fall of the swing. Laughter bubbled out of me in uncontrollable bursts until, out of the corner of my eye, I saw Sherida. Since a body cast covered her from her armpits to her toes, her father stood next to the swing set, holding her up so she could watch.

I only saw Sherida once or twice a year and didn't know her well, but one didn't have to know her well to realize how full of faith and how extraordinarily kind and thoughtful she was. Over the years when our families got together, the rest of us children rode bikes, jumped ropes, and played tag and Red Rover. But Sherida never was able to join us. While we went on to dating and learning to drive a car, doctors put Sherida through medical procedure after medical procedure to try to solve her problems and alleviate her constant, excruciating pain. My mother kept me informed about what Sherida was undergoing, telling me each time she went into the hospital and what the doctors were attempting to do.

As the rest of us grew older and started college, Sherida patiently learned to type with her stiff, deformed hands so that she could find employment. Her mother shared with us how sometimes in the middle of the night she awoke to the sound of Sherida rocking in the rocking chair next to her bed. In too much pain to sleep but not wanting to bother her mother, Sherida would laboriously drag herself into the chair and rock back and forth to try to soothe away the pain. Later as all of us began to marry and have children, Sherida went into the hospital for surgery once more, this time to replace diseased joints with artificial ones. It was a fairly new procedure then, one that gave her much hope for a better future. But there were complications and Sherida died.

Sherida had never broken the Word of Wisdom; in fact, she probably lived it better than most people. So what about the promise my Primary teacher had spoken so much about? Sherida kept the Word of Wisdom, but she couldn't walk. King Benjamin said that if you obey, you will immediately be blessed. But that isn't what I saw or experienced as a young person. I began to notice other examples. People got up in fast and testimony meeting to testify of the miraculous blessings that occurred in their lives from having a son or daughter in the mission field. My parents sent out three missionaries, and each time, all sorts of health and financial problems occurred in our family. I was confused. I could usually see the blessings of obedience, but once in a while they seemed to be missing. King Benjamin said "immediately," and to me this meant "always."

Then one day while studying I found this quote from Bruce R. McConkie: "Faith is a gift of God bestowed as a reward for personal righteousness. It is always given when righteousness is present, and the greater the measure of obedience to God's laws the greater will be the endowment of faith" (McConkie, *Mormon Doctrine*, 264). As I read this passage, suddenly everything made sense to me. Sometimes there are very explicit promises attached to the commandments, such as the promises attached to the

Word of Wisdom, but the immediate blessing King Benjamin spoke of is not always the attached blessing. All who keep the Word of Wisdom will someday walk and run and not be weary, but the immediate blessing of keeping the Word of Wisdom and any other blessing is *increased faith.*

Always and whenever we obey, we are blessed—immediately—with a little more faith. That is how faith grows. And as faith accumulates, we are also blessed with other gifts of the Spirit. The problem is that we don't always see faith increasing or even realize it is happening. But it is. I like to think of it as President Spencer W. Kimball did in the context of the parable of the ten virgins. I imagine that I am one of those women and that every time I am obedient I receive a drop of oil in my lamp. Slowly but surely, the lamp fills with the sustaining oil of faith.

The wondrous thing is how cyclical this process is. Every time we are obedient we are blessed with increased faith, and the more faith we have the easier it is to be obedient. It is like building muscle. When we want to get stronger, we lift weights. At first a ten-pound weight may be difficult to lift, but as our muscles grow stronger from use, the weight becomes easier and easier to lift. Eventually, we try a twenty-pound weight. At first twenty pounds is difficult, but then the muscles grow stronger until twenty pounds is easy. The more weight we lift, the stronger our muscles become, and the stronger our muscles the more we can lift. Obedience and faith work the same way. The more obedient we are, the more faith we have; and the more faith we have, the easier it is to obey.

In his sermon, King Benjamin goes on to say, "I would desire that ye should consider on the blessed and happy state of those that keep the commandments of God" (Mosiah 2:41).

Over the years, I have occasionally pondered what Sherida taught me. While she may not have been able to run in this life, she was full of faith and was happy despite her trials. Now and forevermore she walks and runs with no pain and is not weary. Eventually, all promised blessings are realized. The promises of the gospel are sure. However, the immediate blessing for obedience is often so subtle that it goes unnoticed.

# Only Now

*Take therefore no thought for the morrow: for the morrow shall take thought for the things of itself. Sufficient unto the day is the evil thereof.*

Matthew 6:34

**Live the present moment to the hilt, and do not live in the past or in the future. Success is a journey, not a destination.**

Jacob de Jager, "Service and Happiness," *Ensign*, Nov. 1993, 31

---

I have several friends who love telescopes. They set them up to look at faraway stars or to spot animals in a forest or to peek into other wonders of nature. Telescopes seem almost magical in the way they allow one to not only see into the distance but to see what is absolutely unseeable with the naked eye. Some time ago, I was thinking about this "magic" and began to wish that I had a telescope that instead of seeing into the distance would let me see into the future. Don't you think it would be nice to have a lens that would allow you to see into time like a telescope allows you to see into space?

But before I'd been wishing long, the scripture we started with popped into my head, and I began to think about what I was wanting. When I look through a telescope, I have one eye shut and the other eye up against that little, round eyepiece so that I don't see anything going on around me. While I'm concentrating on nature a mile away, ants are crawling right around my feet, flowers are blooming beside me, people are walking around me, and I don't see any of it. Not only that, but because my attention is focused in the distance, I don't really hear or smell or feel anything near me either. I trade experiencing for merely seeing. When I'm concerned with what is happening "out there," I have no clue what's happening "right here."

I think that's one of the things the Savior is warning us about in this scripture. He's not saying we shouldn't plan for the future, but that we shouldn't *worry* about the future. Many of the modern translations of the New Testament actually change the phrase "take no thought" to "do not worry" or "be not troubled." If we did have an instrument that allowed us to see into the future, chances are many of us would be constantly looking through the apparatus and not noticing what is going on right now. How do I know? Because even without an instrument many of us spend so much time worrying about the future! "What if an accident happens?" or "I just know something terrible is going to happen!" or "I couldn't bear it if such and such happened!" I've often wondered if the last part of the verse "Sufficient unto the day is the evil thereof" isn't almost humorous. To me it means that even if you think of every bad thing that could go wrong, what goes wrong won't be something you've even imagined. Each day has sufficient problems, and your worrying about it isn't going to change a thing.

What the Savior is urging us to do is to let Him worry about the future. He'll take care of it and us. All we need to do is worry about the moment we are in, because it is the only moment we have any control over. President Monson has advised us to "Learn from the past, prepare for the future, live in the present" (Thomas S. Monson, "In Search of Treasure," *Ensign,* May

2003, 22). Think about it. We can't control the future, and we can't change the past. But the good news is that through the Atonement, Jesus Christ can change our past and help us navigate the future.

No matter what we have experienced in the past, it is over and done with. We may have been victimized in the past, but it can only continue to hurt us if we continue to relive it. We may have had glory days in the past, but they are gone and we must move on to other things.

Instead of worrying about what is to come or what has been, all we need concentrate on is whatever we are doing right now. Make the right choice in this moment and the future will take care of itself. Enjoy the freedom this gives you. Let go of the worry. Take your eye off the tiny lens that telescopes you forward or backward, and instead see everything around you. There are 360 degrees of wonder, faith, love, and hope waiting for you—if you just look at *now!*

# Salvation

*Lift up your eyes to the heavens, and look*
*upon the earth beneath; for the heavens shall vanish*
*away like smoke, and the earth shall wax old like*
*a garment; and they that dwell therein shall*
*die in like manner. But my salvation shall be forever,*
*and my righteousness shall not be abolished.*

2 Nephi 8:6

**Man unquestionably has impressive powers . . . But after all our obedience and good works, we cannot be saved from the effects of our sins without the grace extended by the atonement of Jesus Christ . . . Man cannot earn his own salvation.**

Dallin H. Oaks, "What Think Ye of Christ?" *Ensign*, Nov. 1988, 65

Sometimes, especially for those of us who have grown up in the Church, we hear something so much that we no longer think about what we are hearing. With other things, we formed a concept of some principle when we were very young and never stopped as we grew older to evaluate whether we had it right or not. That's what happened to me with the term *salvation*. For me, salvation meant the same thing as redemption and was simply a condition I would live in after death. But because I associated salvation with "live in," it almost took on more of a feeling of place or location than condition.

Then one day as part of my scripture study, I looked up the word *salvation* and had one of those wonderful "a-ha!" moments. The word *salvation* comes from the Latin word *salvus,* from which also come the English words *safe* and *save.* The three words are related and are not about a place at all but about a condition—a condition of safety.

Having safety or being safe means "not exposed to the threat of loss or injury." The Latin *salvus* is related to the Latin word *solidus,* which means "solid"; the Greek word *holos,* which means "whole or safe" (from which we got the word *holy); and the Sanskrit word *sarva,* which means "entire." Discovering salvation as a condition of being solid, whole, safe, and entire gave the term new meaning, but there was even more!

One of the synonyms for *safe* is *secure,* and when I looked up *secure* in the *Visual Thesaurus,* its synonyms surprised me. *Invulnerable, protected, strong, fixed, steady, unattackable, unassailable, inviolable, unafraid, untroubled, assured, firm, protected,* and *sure* were just a few. The word *secure* is formed from the Latin prefix *se-,* meaning "without," and the word *cura,* meaning "care or worry." So being secure is to be without worries, and to be safe or saved is to be without threats, loss, or injury. And salvation is all of the above.

As human beings who once lived with God, our spirits yearn for the safety and security we once knew—a safety difficult to find in a telestial world. The adversary knows how we yearn for security and safety, and since he doesn't want us to find the safety and security that is eternal salvation, he offers hundreds of counterfeit salvations such as wealth, popularity, and education. But as Isaiah explains, all of these attempts at salvation will eventually fail, yet the salvation of the Lord will be forever. "For the moth shall eat them up like a garment, and the worm shall eat them like wool. But my righteousness shall be forever, and my salvation from generation to generation" (2 Ne. 8:8). Don't get me wrong—there is nothing wrong with money, popularity, and intelligence when they are used to do good. But if we are seeking them as ways to make ourselves feel safe and secure, they will fail us. King Benjamin says that following Jesus Christ "is the means whereby salvation cometh. And there is none other salvation save this which hath been spoken of; neither are there any conditions whereby man can be saved except the conditions which I have told you" (Mosiah 4:8).

Just think about it! Because of the Atonement of Jesus Christ we can be rid of such things as fear, worry, regret, trouble, hurt, and distress—*forever.* Jesus Christ has overcome the horrors of sin and death and provided for us a plan of salvation: a plan of safety and security.

# We All Have Hope

*Whoso believeth in God might with*
*surety hope for a better world, yea, even a place at the*
*right hand of God, which hope cometh of faith, maketh*
*an anchor to the souls of men, which would make*
*them sure and steadfast, always abounding in good*
*works, being led to glorify God.*

Ether 12:4

**Hope in our Heavenly Father's merciful plan of happiness leads to peace, mercy, rejoicing, and gladness. The hope of salvation is like a protective helmet; it is the foundation of our faith and an anchor to our souls.**

Dieter F. Uchtdorf, "The Infinite Power of Hope," *Ensign*, Nov. 2008, 21

---

An old Greek myth tells the story of Theseus, who faced the daunting task of entering an elaborate labyrinth, tracking down and slaying the Minotaur, then finding his way back out of the maze. After falling in love with him, the princess Ariadne gives Theseus a golden cord to ensure his safety. Theseus ties the cord to the entrance of the labyrinth and unrolls it as he goes. So, after defeating the Minotaur, instead of being hopelessly lost in the depths of the winding maze, Theseus easily finds his way out by following the golden cord.

This story has some wonderful parallels to life, which often seems like a dangerous labyrinth that is difficult to navigate. But when a golden cord ties us to our eternal destination, the task is not so daunting. And what is our golden cord? Jesus Christ and his teachings.

The prophet Ether tells us that hope is an anchor to the soul (see Ether 12:4). The meaning of that metaphor becomes more poignant when we realize that the Hebrew word often translated as *hope* is *tikvaw*, which means "hope or expectation" but also means *cord*—as in a rope that ties one thing to another. It is easy to see how the word *cord* became associated with the feeling of hope, because when you strongly expect something to happen, so you tie yourself to it. When you are tied to something, you are pulled in that direction. Your hope directs your life. It is your anchor—your stay. When Jesus Christ is our hope, we are tied to Him. He is our anchor. Therefore, hope in Christ is fully expecting to one day be with Him because you are attached to Him.

Being attached to the Savior is a common metaphor throughout the scriptures; the Savior Himself often uses the analogy that He is the bridegroom and His followers are the bride. In English, we say that a bride and groom have "tied the knot." They are attached. They live together. They move from place to place together. They share life's problems and joys together. Their hope is in one another. Going back to the biblical analogy, if we are the bride and Jesus Christ is the groom, we are attached to Him by covenant.

Mormon poses the question, "What is it that ye shall hope for?" and then answers his own question by saying, "Ye shall have hope through the Atonement of Christ and the power of his resurrection, to be raised unto life eternal, and this because of your faith in him according to the promise" (Moroni 7:41).

Every human being has placed his or her hope in something. It seems to be a human condition that we can't go through life or even through a day without hope. Some of us place our hope in wealth—we think that if we have enough money we will be saved from life's problems, that if we can buy whatever we want we will be happy. Some of us place our hope in intelligence—we think that if we are smarter or more educated than everyone around us we will get the good jobs, will always have the answers, and will be respected. Some people place their hope in popularity, thinking that if enough people love and adore them they will always be safe and secure and happy. Others place their hope in being "with it" or "cool." They feel that if  they decorate their homes with what is currently in style, or wear the right clothes, or follow all the current rules of etiquette, they will be accepted and admired and will be safe in social situations.

Some people even place their hope in negative things, thinking that if they can be intimidating or manipulative enough they will always be able to bully their way to what they want—to the things that make them feel safe and secure. The prophet Isaiah takes us back to our imagery of the cord as hope when he warns, "Woe unto them that draw iniquity with cords of vanity, and sin as it were with a cart rope" (Isa. 5:18). In this verse, Isaiah gives us a vivid picture of mortals who constantly drag heavy carts of sin behind them, clinging to the cord that pulls the cart of sin. The cord is their vanity, their pride is their hope, and they cling to that cord stubbornly. They are too proud to admit they have been wrong, too vain to undergo the humbling process of repentance. Instead, they labor with the heavy load, hoping that if they can drag it long enough something will change. But perhaps the saddest negative hope is found in suicidal people, who place their hope in the fact that death will help them escape their problems and bring them to a place of safety.

There are hundreds of things people place their hope in, and many of them do provide temporary safety and security, but there is only one cord of hope that will bring eternal salvation, and that is hope in Jesus Christ. When we attach ourselves to the Savior and firmly expect that He will lead us to salvation, we have true hope. That expectation is a cord that will securely tie us to all that is good for time and all eternity.

# Connecting with Heaven

*Pray always, and I will pour out my Spirit upon*
*you, and great shall be your blessing—yea, even more*
*than if you should obtain treasures of earth and*
*corruptibleness to the extent thereof.*

Doctrine and Covenants 19:38

**From simple trials to our Gethsemanes, prayer can put
us in touch with God, our greatest source of comfort
and counsel.**

Ezra Taft Benson, "Do Not Despair," *Ensign*, Nov. 1974, 65

Recently, I had the opportunity to spend a night at our stake Young Women's camp. As we sat around a blazing bonfire, the bishop of our ward took the girls on a spiritual "hike" through the scriptures, exploring verses concerning prayer. Line upon line, he showed the girls what prayer is and how it should operate in our lives. After he finished, the girls were invited to share their testimonies. Many of them spoke of prayer, recalling instances when they had lost something or were in dire need so they prayed and their prayers were answered, often in very miraculous ways.

As I sat listening to the girls, I watched the brightly burning fire send smoke high into the sky as if it connected earth to the stars. As I watched it swirl upward, I began to think about the symbolic significance of smoke. My mind wandered to thoughts of the tabernacle that traveled with the children of Israel when Moses led them through the wilderness. In my imagination I could see the small altar that stood in front of the veil that led into the Holy of Holies. On this altar the priests burned incense as part of their holy rituals, sending smoke heavenward just like the smoke from this fire. The symbolism of the smoke rising is an easy symbol to understand. It served to remind the people of the importance of prayer, which connects us earthbound mortals to God.

As the young women of my ward told their stories of prayer, I thought of the many, many times God had answered my prayers—prayers where I asked for help with rather trivial things, and prayers asking for miracles when my children were ill or in need. My prayers had been answered, and I knew that prayer was a precious opportunity to communicate directly with God.

However, several months previously, I had experienced prayer in a different way when my father passed away. My sister, mother, and I were there that morning, and as soon as he died we called my two brothers who lived nearby. Within minutes they were at the house. The hospice nurse who had cared for my father told us that before he called the mortuary we could take all the time we wanted with Dad. So we gathered around the bed where Dad's body lay. Then, as we had done so many, many times in our growing up years, we knelt around Mom and Dad's bed and prayed. My brother was voice, and he poured out his heart in thanks that we had been blessed to be a family. He thanked God for the love we shared. He prayed for our mother, who after almost sixty years of marriage to Dad would be left alone. But most of all he thanked God for this man who had taught us the gospel of Jesus Christ and loved and cared for us all our lives.

As we knelt and listened to the words of the prayer, the Spirit filled the room and our hearts. I felt my heart lifted like smoke rising. I felt connected to heaven in a way I had never experienced before in my life. The feelings of joy and peace that filled me are not normally part of this telestial world; they belong to another world. And yet, in that moment of prayer, we were privileged to be part of that other world. We were connected to heaven, and since that moment my prayers have been different. Instead of simply communicating, I'm striving to connect.

As I watched the blazing fire at girl's camp, the realization hit me that before Dad's death, smoke was a symbol I understood intellectually to represent prayer. Now I understood from someplace deep within my bones that prayer can lift us out of this world and connect us to God.

# Prayer

*Confess your faults one to another, and pray one for another, that ye may be healed. The effectual fervent prayer of a righteous man availeth much.*

James 5:16

**Christ taught the Nephites that prayer is more than just a means to receive our Father in Heaven's generosity; rather, prayer itself is an act of faith as well as an act of righteousness. Prayer is the defining act of the worshipper of God the Father and His Son Jesus Christ. This is because the act of prayer itself can change and purify us, both individually and as a group.**

David E. Sorensen, "Prayer," *Ensign*, May 1993, 30

The original meaning of the word *pray* was to "obtain by entreaty." The modern definition is "a petition to God in word or thought." The Bible Dictionary modifies this by explaining that "the object of prayer is not to change the will of God, but to secure for ourselves and for others blessings that God is already willing to grant, but that are made conditional on our asking for them" (Bible Dictionary, "Prayer," 753). Thus, asking and entreating God are an important part of prayer. But for Latter-day Saints a better definition of prayer would simply be "communication with God," because prayer is so much more than entreating or asking or petitioning. Prayer is also about sharing honest feelings, giving thanks, and being nurtured spiritually.

It is also beneficial to realize that prayer as communication with God is a two-way communication. Too often when we pray, the word *amen* takes on the feeling of the racer's command "Ready, set, go." As soon as the *amen* is said, we jump up and run. Think about it. How would you like your child to come to you and pour out his or her heart, ask for answers to pertinent questions, ask for things needed, and then turn around and run out the door before you could open your mouth to answers? And yet so often that's what we do to our Heavenly Father.

In order to make prayer more meaningful, we taught our children that after praying they should remain on their knees for a few minutes to listen and feel what their Father in Heaven wanted them to know. I'll never forget one night as I was putting five-year-old Anissa to bed and began to review this principle with her. "Now after you pray," I began, "wait a few . . ."

She didn't let me finish. She put her little hand over my mouth and said, "Mom, you don't need to tell me that because once when I listened Heavenly Father said, 'I love you.'"

As President Hinckley stated, "What a marvelous and wonderful thing is prayer. Think of it. We can actually speak with our Father in Heaven. He will hear and respond, but we need to listen to that response. Nothing is too serious and nothing too unimportant to share with Him" (Gordon B. Hinckley, "Stay on the High Road," *Ensign*, May 2004, 114).

But prayer isn't always uttered when we are on our knees. I have a friend who came upon this verse in the Doctrine and Covenants: "Yea, I tell thee, that thou mayest know that there is none else save God that knowest thy thoughts and the intents of thy heart" (6:16). She said that as she read these words, a realization burst like lightning in her mind. Every thought she thought was communication with God! He was the only one who could hear and know her thoughts, and therefore every thought was, in essence, a prayer.

The realization that prayer isn't just formal, on-your-knees-communication changed her life. She began to watch her thoughts carefully and to make sure  they were appropriate for God to hear. And because she was constantly acknowledging that God could hear her, she felt closer to Him and sensed His presence in her life more often.

But we can expand our definition even more as we come to realize that our very life is a prayer. This is what Adam learned from an angel. After being driven from Eden, Adam built an altar, where he worshipped and offered sacrifices to the Lord. One day after Adam worshipped in this way, an angel appeared to him and taught him. One of the angel's instructions was "Thou shalt do all that thou doest in the name of the son" (Moses 4:8). Imagine living your life so that all you do and say could be done in the name of Christ. A life like that would be a prayer. It is what we should all be striving for.

In short, the definition of prayer is summed up by words from a beloved hymn: "Prayer is the Christian's vital breath, The Christian's native air" ("Prayer Is the Soul's Sincere Desire," *Hymns*, no. 145).

# A Letter from Home

*Fear thou not; for I am with thee: be not
dismayed; for I am thy God: I will strengthen thee;
yea, I will help thee; yea, I will uphold thee with
the right hand of my righteousness.*

Isaiah 41:10

**You have as great an opportunity for satisfaction in the
performance of your duty as I do in mine. The progress
of this work will be determined by our joint efforts.
Whatever your calling, it is as fraught with the same
kind of opportunity to accomplish good as is mine.
What is really important is that this is the work of the
Master. Our work is to go about doing good as did He.**

Gordon B. Hinckley, "This Is the Work of the Master," *Ensign*, May 1995, 69

---

Shortly after Lehi and Nephi left Jerusalem, the Babylonians swept through the Holy Land, destroyed the country, and took captive the most able and talented Jews. During this time the prophet Jeremiah wrote a letter in the name of the Lord to instruct and encourage the exiles who had been taken from their homes to Babylon. The letter reads:

*To all the exiles whom I have sent into exile from Jerusalem to
Babylon: Build houses and live in them; plant gardens and eat
what they produce. Take wives and have sons and daughters; take*

*wives for your sons, and give your daughters in marriage, that they may bear sons and daughters; multiply there, and do not decrease. But seek the welfare of the city where I have sent you into exile, and pray to the Lord on its behalf, for in its welfare you will find your welfare. For thus says the Lord of hosts, the God of Israel: Do not let the prophets and the diviners who are among you deceive you, and do not listen to the dreams that they dream, for it is a lie that they are prophesying to you in my name; I did not send them, says the Lord. For thus says the Lord: Only when Babylon's seventy years are completed will I visit you, and I will fulfill to you my promise and bring you back to this place. For surely I know the plans I have for you, says the Lord, plans for your welfare and not for harm, to give you a future with hope.* (NRSV Jer. 29:4–11)

I love this letter and like to read it as if it were a letter from God directly to me. After all, I am also an exile. I have been exiled from my heavenly home and am wandering in this strange, foreign place of adversity and trial called a telestial world, just as these Jews were taken from Jerusalem into Babylon.

When one reads the letter in this way, the symbolism becomes even more poignant. While there is no agreement on the correct translation, some scholars believe the name *Jerusalem* means "founded peaceful." Whatever the meaning, we do know it is a promised and holy land. In contrast, the name *Babylon* comes from the word *babel* and refers to a city of materialism and sensual pleasure. Symbolically, Babylon is the telestial world we live in. Thus the exiles have been taken from a holy place and forced to live in Babylon until "seventy years are completed."

This is interesting because the numbers seven, seventy, and seven hundred are all symbols of completion or perfection.

What the Lord is saying, then, is that the exiles will have to dwell in Babylon until the time is completed, and then He will visit them. And they aren't just to bide their time but are to make the best of their situation. They are to have families and to work to make Babylon a better place, and they are to pray for its welfare. But they are to be cautious about the false prophets in Babylon who might lead them astray. What better advice for those of us exiled in this mortal world!

Therefore, when we read our letter from the Lord, we receive three instructions:

1. Make the best of whatever situation you are in. As an exile from heaven, you should build, plant, and do what you can to create goodness wherever you can, for in making this world a better place to live, you will be happy.

2. Do not pay attention to the false teachers and others in Babylon who try to lead you astray.

3. Never give up hope, because when the time of trial and testing is completed, God will rescue you. He has wonderful plans for you. Nothing you encounter will permanently harm you. Instead, the Lord is planning a way for you to fare well, and He desires to give you a future with hope.

# Atonement

*Now Aaron began to open the scriptures
unto them concerning the coming of Christ, and also
concerning the resurrection of the dead, and that there
could be no redemption for mankind save it
were through the death and sufferings of Christ,
and the atonement of his blood.*

Alma 21:9

So as I conceive it, we must stand adamant for the doctrine of the atonement of Jesus the Christ, for the divinity of his conception, for his sinless life, and for, shall I say, the divinity of his death, his voluntary surrender of life. He was not killed, he gave up his life. It is our mission, perhaps the most fundamental purpose of our work, to bear constant testimony of Jesus the Christ. We must never permit to enter into our thoughts and certainly not into our teachings, the idea that he was merely a great teacher, a great philosopher, the builder of a great system of ethics.

J. Reuben Clark, *Conference Report*, Oct. 1955, 23

The Atonement is the miracle that changes us—dirty and stained with sin—into purified people worthy to enter the presence of God. We keep the commandments so that we are in a position for the miracle to take place in our lives, and then Jesus

Christ does the rest. We can't do it ourselves. No matter how hard we try, no matter what we do, we can't make that miracle happen. Only Jesus Christ can do it for us. But too many of us go through life thinking we have to do it all. Those thoughts can be nothing but discouraging.

To understand better, let's look closely at words used to represent the concept of atonement. In English, the word *atonement* means "reparation for an offense or injury." It is an old English word composed of two words, *at* and *one,* added to the suffix *–ment.* The suffix means "process of," so when we put the words together, the result means "the process of becoming one." Specifically, *atonement* is the process of becoming one with Jesus Christ. This oneness occurs because Jesus Christ satisfies our debt and thus qualifies us to be saved.

In the Old Testament, the word *atonement* appears 69 times. In Hebrew, the word is *kaphar,* which means "to cover or purge." It is closely related to the noun that is translated *pitch* in the story of Noah. In that account, Noah is told to cover the ark with *kopher.* I love the visual image that gives me of the Atonement. Noah was working with hand tools. Imagine the unevenness of each board and how difficult it would be to make the boards fit together tight enough so that water wouldn't seep in. In addition, lumber contains knots and other defects that weaken the boards and allow water to seep in. But when covered in pitch, the defects disappear, the gaps between the boards are sealed up, and the ship becomes seaworthy.

Likewise, Jesus Christ makes us "seaworthy." Because He atoned for our sins, our vessel is sailable, and it won't sink. And if we follow the correct course outlined on the map (the scriptures), we can return to God and live with Him for eternity.

In the Greek from which our New Testament was translated, the word for *atonement* is *katallage.* But the word only appears in one verse of the entire New Testament. That verse is Romans 5:11: "And not only so, but we also joy in God through our Lord Jesus Christ, by whom we have now received the atonement" (Romans 5:11). *Katallage* zeroes in on another facet of the Atonement. It means "exchange," as in the exchange of money. It also means "adjustment of a difference, reconciliation, and restoration to favour." These last definitions are close to the English meaning. But the first definition—the idea of exchange—is what intrigues me. The Atonement is a transaction whereby Jesus Christ has paid for our sins and in exchange asks us to come to Him by living the commandments.

This idea of the Atonement as exchange brings us back to the fact that the Atonement is a miracle. In Gethsemane and on Calvary, Jesus Christ became us and offered us the opportunity to become like Him.

# Redeemed!

*Thou art angry, O Lord, with this people, because
they will not understand thy mercies which thou hast
bestowed upon them because of thy Son.*

Alma 33:16

**When we begin to understand the magnitude of [the
Messiah's] sacrifice and service to us individually and
collectively, we then cannot consider anything else to be
of more importance or to approach His significance in
our lives. For most of us, this understanding does not
come all at once and likely will not be fully complete
during our mortal sojourn. We do know, however, that
as we learn line upon line, our appreciation for the
Savior's contributions will increase and our knowledge
and assurance of their truthfulness will grow.**

Cecil O. Samuelson Jr., "Perilous Times," *Ensign*, Nov. 2004, 50–51

When I was checking out at the grocery store one time, the
clerk asked, "Do you have any coupons to redeem?" I'd
heard the word *redeemed* used in that way before, but suddenly
my mind spun with the fact that *redeemed* was used for one of the
most trivial experiences in my life—the use of a piece of paper
in order to save ten cents—and the most significant event in the
history of mankind—the saving of my soul.

That experience sent me to my dictionary to explore the
word and all its connotations. The simple synonym we usually

associate with *redeemed* is the word *saved,* which we discussed when we talked about salvation. Jesus Christ did save us, but if we let the meaning of redemption stop there, the significance eludes us. My dictionary says that to *redeem* is "to buy back: to repurchase: to get or win back." The insinuation is that if something is repurchased it must have first belonged to someone and then been sold away or lost. The fact that we are redeemed indicates that we were once God's, but because of the Fall, we needed to be bought or won back. We are His! And even though we were lost, He loved us enough to go to great effort and cost to regain us.

The second definition adds even more feeling to this concept. It states that to redeem is "to free from what distresses or harms: to free from captivity by payment of ransom: to extricate from or help to overcome something detrimental: to free from the consequences of sin." Certainly, all of these apply to the condition we are in because of the Fall and Atonement—to the ultimate saving of our souls. But they also indicate that redeeming isn't something that applies only on the day we "check out."

To *redeem* also means "to change for the better; to reform; to repair; to restore." The process of being changed from a natural and carnal person to a spiritual being is a change for the better, a reformation that could not take place without the Atonement of Jesus Christ. Therefore, it is a daily process. Daily, God helps us to overcome something. Daily, He releases us from the consequences of sin if we repent. Daily, He frees us from distress and harm if we turn to Him. Daily, He redeems us.

Because of the redemption offered us by Jesus Christ, each day of our lives we can be repaired, restored a little more until at last we are restored to Him eternally. We are healed of all the hurt and sorrow and defects of mortality. We are repaired!

In a General Conference talk, Bishop Richard C. Edgley expressed my own feelings of joy for this concept of redemption when he said, "My heart throbs with the knowledge that Jesus Christ is my personal Savior and that His love for me was sufficient that He would suffer unimaginable pain and even death. My heart throbs when in the solitude of my deep thoughts I realize I can be cleansed, purified, and redeemed through the blood of Jesus Christ. My heart throbs when I contemplate the price that was paid—the suffering incurred to spare me of similar personal suffering for my sins and transgressions" (Richard C. Edgley, "A Still, Small Voice and a Throbbing Heart," *Ensign*, May 2005, 10).

As fantastic as this is, it isn't all there is to this concept. One more definition for *redeem* is "to atone for; expiate; to offset the bad effect of." That sounds like the best of Sunday School lessons, but it continues with a phrase I've never heard connected with those lessons. In the Merrian-Webster Online Dictionary, the last definition of *redeem* is "to make worthwhile." Because of the Atonement of the Savior, my life has been made worthwhile.

What I learned from my studies is that redemption is about more than being saved. Redemption is about life being changed from worthless to worthwhile. And it is about *being*—our being what God is.

# Power from Small Things

*A very large ship is benefited very much by a
very small helm in the time of a storm, by being kept
workways with the wind and the waves.*

Doctrine and Covenants 123:16

**I have always found that when we do the little things
correctly, the Lord gives us the strength to accomplish
big things. . . . You might not always understand the
reasons for some rules or commandments, but if you
will follow them even in the little things you will have
more strength to do big things. . . . And you will have
the great blessing of knowing that you are on the Lord's
side and that He is on yours.**

Donald L. Hallstrom, "Friend to Friend: On the Lord's Side," *Friend*, Sept. 2002, 8

It is a simple yet profound principle in economics that if you
take care of the pennies, the dollars take care of themselves.
That principle works in spiritual things also. There are certain
commandments that when observed carefully pave the way for
all other righteousness. It is interesting how this is pointed out in
the Ten Commandments.

The Ten Commandments are included twice in the Old
Testament: once in Exodus 20 and once in Deuteronomy 5. Both
accounts begin with a reminder that God brought the people
out of bondage in the land of Egypt. This can be read as a
metaphor because the commandments that follow are designed

to bring us out of spiritual bondage.

Six of the Ten Commandments are almost identical in the two acccunts, and these six are explained in a total of only 57 words—an average of 9.5 words per commandment. However, the Lord uses more than four times as many words to explain the remaining four commandments—240 words in Exodus and 295 in Deuteronomy. These four commandments include: "Thou shalt not make unto thee any graven image," "Remember the sabbath day, to keep it holy," "Honor thy father and thy mother," and "Thou shalt not covet" (Ex. 20:4, 8, 12, 17).

As mortals we tend to think that the "bigger" laws concern murder and adultery and theft. But it should make us stop and wonder when we see where the Lord spent the majority of His instruction. To explain the importance of not worshipping graven images, 91 words are used in the Exodus account, and 90 in Deuteronomy. The command regarding Sabbath observance comprises 94 words in Exodus and 133 in Deuteronomy. The commandment to honor parents is explained in 22 words in Exodus and 38 in Deuteronomy. And the command not to covet is detailed in 33 words in Exodus and 34 in Deuteronomy.

To me, this emphasis indicates that if I refuse to worship graven images (which in our day involve such things as materialism), if I keep the Sabbath day holy, honor my parents, and refuse to be jealous and covet what others have, I won't have much problem with such things as killing, lying, stealing, or adultery. But there is something more. When we compare the Exodus and Deuteronomy accounts we find that of these four commandments, three—those dealing with graven images, honoring parents, and coveting—are explained in almost exactly the same way in both books of scripture. But the law of the Sabbath is explained very differently in Exodus than in Deuteronomy. This gives even more emphasis to the commandment to keep the Sabbath day holy, thus stressing its importance.

The Exodus account reads, "Remember the sabbath day, to keep it holy. Six days shalt thou labour, and do all thy work: But the seventh day is the sabbath of the Lord thy God: in it thou shalt not do any work, thou, nor thy son, nor thy daughter, thy manservant, nor thy maidservant, nor thy cattle, nor thy stranger that is within thy gates: For in six days the Lord made heaven and earth, the sea, and all that in them is, and rested the seventh day: wherefore the Lord blessed the sabbath day, and hallowed it" (Exodus 20:8–11). God created the world for us. It is designed to nurture, delight, and benefit us. Just as light, water, and vegetation are necessary for our physical bodies, observing sacred time is necessary for the nurturing and growth of the spiritual body. In other words, in the Exodus account, God is helping us understand that the Sabbath is necessary for our spiritual life. It is a time to pay close attention to the divinity within us and to nurture that divinity with the power that is inherent in sacred time.

The Deuteronomy account repeats the particulars of the commandment, but instead of explaining the Sabbath connection to the creation of the world, it states, "Remember that thou wast a servant in the land of Egypt, and that the Lord thy God brought thee out thence through a mighty hand and by a stretched out arm: therefore the Lord thy God commanded thee to keep the sabbath day" (Deut. 5:15). The emphasis here is on the fact that by keeping the Sabbath day holy we will be delivered out of spiritual bondage just as the children of Israel were delivered out of physical bondage.

Sometimes we tend to subconsciously divide the commandments into the "big ones" and the "little ones" and think that breaking the "little ones" isn't all that bad. But the Lord puts emphasis on the "little" things, and as Elder Pinegar warns, "Big problems grow out of thinking that little things don't matter" (Rex D. Pinegar, "The Simple Things," *Ensign,* Nov. 1994, 80).

There is a message in this. When we focus on living the simple commandments, we discover that they empower us to do all that we need to do to return to our Father in Heaven.

# There's Help for the Journey

*Take my yoke upon you, and learn*
*of me; for I am meek and lowly in heart: and*
*ye shall find rest unto your souls.*

Matthew 11:29

**Many carry heavy burdens. Some have lost a loved one to death or care for one who is disabled. Some have been wounded by divorce. Others yearn for an eternal marriage. Some are caught in the grip of addictive substances or practices like alcohol, tobacco, drugs, or pornography. Others have crippling physical or mental impairments. Some are challenged by same-gender attraction. Some have terrible feelings of depression or inadequacy. In one way or another, many are heavy laden. To each of us our Savior gives this loving invitation: "Come unto me, all ye that labour and are heavy laden, and I will give you rest."**

Dallin H. Oaks, "He Heals the Heavy Laden," *Ensign*, Nov. 2006, 6

---

When I was in grade school, we celebrated a field day at the end of every school year. That day consisted of races like the fifty-yard dash, a wheelbarrow race, a relay race, and a three-legged race. All year I looked forward to field day, and when the day arrived I participated in as many events as I could. But I had forgotten all about field day until a student recently asked me: "I understand how taking the Savior's yoke upon me would be beneficial, but how do I do it? How can I yoke myself with Christ?"

Running three-legged races on my grade-school field days was the closest I'd ever come to being physically yoked to anyone or anything, and my student's question sent me flying back through the years to the feeling of having my leg belted to someone else's leg. Standing normally with our arms at our sides didn't work. We needed to be more "connected" or we got in each other's way. If you were shy or reticent or didn't know the other person well, this was awkward, because unless arms were around each other you couldn't balance—let alone work in tandem. Therefore, we always found a partner for the race that we knew well enough to be comfortable embracing.

But balance wasn't the only problem! I remember the awkwardness as we tried to move. I had to sense when she was starting to move and in what direction she was moving, and she had to know when and where I moved. We could use verbal commands, but the intuitive sensing was much more valuable. Verbal commands were often too late or too soon or misunderstood. Intuitive feelings always came at the exact moment they were needed.

It didn't take long to realize that unless we were totally in sync with one another, we tumbled to the ground, and if we tumbled, getting upright while lashed together was quite a feat. Usually, if we fell we couldn't finish the race, let alone win it. To accomplish the goal of crossing the finish line, we both had to focus on each other. We had to be totally present in the situation. We couldn't daydream or be distracted by what others were doing or thoughts of how the race went last year. We had to be fully aware of the present and of each other's every move and intention in that present.

As these field-day memories came to mind, I realized how much they applied to being yoked with Christ. In order to help in His work and to allow Him to help pull my load, I need to be focused in the present. Too often as mortal beings we spend our time reliving the past or dreaming about the future and not really living our life at all. Instead, it passes by while we are thinking about something else. But if my mind is not here now, who is living my life? Who is making the decisions that matter in this moment? Who is listening for and receiving the inspiration from the Spirit that is necessary for me right now? Who is experiencing the joy in this moment?

As I thought on this, I realized that being yoked with Christ means being focused on the present so that I can feel and receive inspiration—inspiration that tells me when I need to turn, how to balance, when I need to go straight ahead, and what pace to set so that I don't stumble before the finish line. In addition I realized that if I am yoked with Christ, when life presents me with a problem, I simply follow His lead and confront the problem. My mind doesn't wander into fear of what is going to happen or wade through memories of past adversity. Instead, I stay present so I can sense the inspiration of the Spirit and do what the Spirit tells me to do.

Living in the present and being yoked with Christ, we naturally move with Him. We turn left when He turns left. We turn right when He turns right. We follow His pace. We stop when He stops. It is very simple if we follow Christ's lead. It is a matter of being in tune with each moment, of being here NOW in order to follow His lead. Our minds aren't stressed about what needs to be done tomorrow or next week. He'll tell us when it is time. We aren't distracted with thoughts of what happened last week, last year, or in our childhood. We just do what we need to do now—what Christ, through the Spirit, guides us to do.

On the other hand, even if we intend to be yoked with Christ, when we confront difficulties and our minds are not present, we don't sense what we are to do. We stumble over the very things that are intended to guide and help us. We not only pull the load of adversity, but we pull *against* the Savior instead of *with* Him. We are deciding which direction to move and how fast to move and what to do along the way. That is extremely difficult when we have never trodden the path before. As we decide how to do this, our mind depends on a gamut of memories and fears. We bring all our past difficulties into the present situation, so that in reality we aren't yoked to Christ but are yoked to our fears and forebodings. We think things such as: "Well, last time something bad like this happened it was horrendous," "Because such and such happened in my past, I'm not equipped to handle this new situation," "This could keep such and such from happening in the future," "What is tomorrow going to be like because of this?" and "My whole future is ruined." In this way, the difficulty becomes an all-encompassing emotional experience that weaves itself not only into the mind, but into the muscles, heart, and bones of the body. (You can actually feel it tightening your stomach into knots!) Hence, the difficulty is forever part of you, and what is part of you tends to define you.

But when we are yoked with Christ, only the present matters. We sense what needs to be done by following the lead of the Savior and the promptings of the Spirit. Calm in the fact that we are yoked with Him, we concentrate on the present. We know exactly how to deal with the problem—we just stay focused on

Him. Then, like water encountering a rock in the stream, we are guided around the problem. The beauty of this isn't just that the problem is solved much more easily. The beauty is that because we are focused on Christ instead of the problem, it never becomes a part of us. When we are yoked with Christ, we are living our lives instead of being controlled by our circumstances.

# The Sacrament

*Assemble yourselves upon the land of Zion;
and hold a meeting and rejoice together, and offer a
sacrament unto the Most High.*

Doctrine and Covenants 62:4

**To follow the Savior requires us to know who He is—the Son of God—to take His name upon us, to remember His atoning sacrifice, and to keep His commandments. We made these covenants at baptism, and we renew our baptismal covenants each time we partake of the sacrament.**

Robert D. Hales, "Fulfilling Our Duty to God," *Ensign*, Nov. 2001, 38

According to the *Oxford English Dictionary*, a sacrament is "a Christian rite that is believed to have been ordained by Christ and held to be a means of divine grace or to be a sign or symbol of a spiritual reality." Like most of our religious words, the word *sacrament* comes to us from Latin. *Sacrament* originally referred to an oath of allegiance or obligation, and was derived from the Latin *sacrare*, which means "to consecrate." In the Church, the word has come to be used for one specific thing: the sacrament of the bread and wine that the Savior initiated during the Last Supper.

One Sunday during the ordinance of the sacrament, I looked in my scriptures and noticed a new connection in the phrases on the prayer on the water. The semicolon after the words *shed for them* had always caused me to pause. But that day I read the words without the semicolon and realized that there was more meaning in those words than just a list of happenings. The words can also mean that because the blood of the Son was shed for me, I can witness unto God. Without the Atonement of Jesus Christ I could not be a witness for righteousness. I could not do what I had covenanted to do when I partook of the bread. I began to realize more fully how terribly dark, lonely, impossible, and despairing life would be if there had been no Atonement.

As Lehi explained to his son Jacob, "O the wisdom of God, his mercy and grace! For behold, if the flesh should rise no more our spirits must become subject to that angel who fell from before the presence of the Eternal God, and became the devil, to rise no more. And our spirits must have become like unto him, and we become devils, angels to a devil, to be shut out from the presence of our God, and to remain with the father of lies, in misery, like unto himself; yea, to that being who beguiled our first parents, who transformeth himself nigh unto an angel of light, and stirreth up the children of men unto secret combinations of murder and all manner of secret works of darkness" (2 Ne. 9:8–9).

Without the Atonement I would not have access to the Spirit. There would be no such things as peace, joy, and happiness. If none of those things were there for me to experience and gain a testimony from, I would not be able to bear witness of the gospel. And I wouldn't have the power to learn and grow and change so that my life itself would witness that Jesus is the Christ. Without the Atonement I would be unable to witness on a weekly basis that I am willing to take the Son's name upon myself.

But because of Jesus Christ the bonds of both misery and

death have been broken. Because of Jesus Christ I can go each Sunday to the sacrament altar and renew my baptismal covenants. I can reinforce my efforts to do better and to be better. Because of Jesus Christ I have access to the divine grace that makes witnessing Him a spiritual reality.

# The Gift of the Sabbath

*The inhabitants of Zion shall also observe*
*the Sabbath day to keep it holy.*

Doctrine and Covenants 68:29

**Our observance or nonobservance of the Sabbath is an unerring measure of our attitude toward the Lord personally and toward his suffering in Gethsemane, his death on the cross, and his resurrection from the dead. It is a sign of whether we are Christians in very deed, or whether our conversion is so shallow that commemoration of his atoning sacrifice means little or nothing to us.**

Mark E. Petersen, "The Sabbath Day," *Ensign*, May 1975, 49

In addition to sacred places like temples and chapels, God has given us the great blessing of sacred time—the Sabbath. In Old Testament days, the Sabbath was celebrated on the seventh day of the week, but after the resurrection of the Lord, which took place on the first day of the week, early Christians began to celebrate the Sabbath on Sunday.

In Exodus 20:11 we are told that "the Lord blessed the Sabbath day, and hallowed it," which means He made it holy. These aren't just words. If you "listen" carefully you can feel the difference between Sunday and the rest of the days of the week. I love to wake up a little early Sunday morning, roll over, and soak in the warm feeling. It isn't a matter of weather—it can be stormy or cold, but Sundays are "sunnier." Just as a detectable difference exists in the air between spring and autumn, there is a detectable difference in the atmosphere on the Sabbath. If you pay attention, you discover that a sense of rejoicing and joy penetrates the air. When you breathe in deeply, you can feel it become part of you.

On the Sabbath, peace and calm whisper reassurance into my very being. Because of this feeling, I eagerly anticipate the Sabbath all week long.

When God "hallowed" the Sabbath, He set it apart for holy use. Our responsibility isn't to make it holy but to *keep* it holy. Holy means "divine, or devoted entirely to the work of deity." Too often we define the Sabbath by explaining what can't be done in it, thereby generating negative feelings about this special day. But sacred time is a time to celebrate. The Hebrew word for the Sabbath, *shabbath,* comes from the verb *shabath,* which means "to cease, desist, or rest." Think about that for a minute. So much of life is focused on doing and acquiring that we lose sight of what is important. The Sabbath exists to give us rest from the stress of making a living and worrying about ourselves and all the things that need to be done.

So much of our time is consumed with working to provide the physical necessities of life that time itself tends to take on a negative feeling. Time is so fleeting—so unforgiving—and since it is so easily lost we tend to covet it. We want more time for ourselves. But time isn't used only to provide for physical life. Time is a necessary component of spiritual life. By creating sacred time, God gave us a break in the physical battle. This break in our schedule allows us to forget about worldly things and immerse ourselves in the things of God—to symbolically enter His presence. It has been noted that when men forget about God they don't stop worshiping; instead, they just change what they worship. They begin to worship earthly things such as food, clothing, shelter, and pleasure—the things that sustain physical life. Therefore, how we spend the sacred time of the Sabbath is an indication of what we worship.

In answering the question, "Why has God asked us to honor the Sabbath day?", Elder James E. Faust said, "It has to do with the need for regeneration and the strengthening of our spiritual being. God knows that, left completely to our own devices without regular reminders of our spiritual needs, many would degenerate into the preoccupation of satisfying earthly desires and appetites. This need for physical, mental, and spiritual regeneration is met in large measure by faithful observance of the Sabbath day" (James E. Faust, "The Lord's Day," *Ensign,* Nov. 1991, 33).

People often acknowledge the encouragement and empowerment that comes from being in holy places such as temples. That same power and encouragement is available when we savor holy time in holy ways. There is a divinity within us—the light of Christ—that guides us beyond the things of this world and to the things of God. If we pay attention to it, we are also entitled to use the gift of the Holy Ghost to help us find holy ways to use holy time. Elder Faust stated, "What is worthy or unworthy on the Sabbath day will have to be judged by each of us by trying to be honest with the Lord. On the Sabbath day we should do what we have to do and what we ought to do in an attitude of worshipfulness and then limit our other activities" (ibid).

As we endeavor to spend our holy time in holy ways, we

realize that the Sabbath symbolically represents the rest entered into after our mortal struggle. Alma said in the Book of Mormon, "Whosoever repenteth, and hardeneth not his heart, he shall have claim on mercy through mine Only Begotten Son, unto a remission of his sins; and these shall enter into my rest" (Alma 12:34).

Entering into the rest or Shabbat of the Lord is entering a permanent sacred place and permanent sacred time where the struggles, worries, and fears of mortality are no more. The Sabbath is meant to give us a taste of the rest that is heaven. But it will only be heavenly if we rest from our worldly endeavors and partake of the holiness that is the Sabbath.

# Truth and Revelation

*Again I say unto you that if ye will enter in*
*by the way, and receive the Holy Ghost, it will show*
*unto you all things what ye should do.*

2 Nephi 32:5

**I will tell you a rule by which you may know the Spirit of God from the spirit of evil. The Spirit of God always produces joy and satisfaction of mind. When you have that Spirit you are happy; when you have another spirit you are not happy. The spirit of doubt is the spirit of the evil one; it produces uneasiness and other feelings that interfere with happiness and peace.**

George Q. Cannon, *Journal of Discourses*, 26 vols. (Salt Lake City: Deseret Book Co., 1873), 15:375

---

I've often pondered how revelation technically works. For example, I've wondered whether the Spirit simply prompts us once in a while or if He is always speaking to us. I don't know for sure, but judging from the scripture above, it seems to me that the Spirit must be speaking to us all of the time, prompting, guiding, teaching, warning, and comforting us. If we are in tune, we receive what is given to us. If we are not in tune, we don't. I imagine it is something like a radio station that is broadcasting twenty-four hours a day, seven days a week. If our radio is tuned to the station, we hear the things we need to. We receive the comfort and knowledge we need. If our radio is turned off or tuned to another frequency or is picking up some kind of static interference, we don't hear what is broadcast.

Thinking about it in this way motivates me to stay in tune and keeps me on guard against static that can keep me from receiving good, clear reception. One of the great causes of static, I have discovered, has to do with truth. The Spirit only deals in truth. In Jacob 4:13 we are told that "the Spirit speaketh the truth and lieth not. Wherefore, it speaketh of things as they really are, and of things as they really will be; wherefore, these things are manifested unto us plainly, for the salvation of our souls."

In the Doctrine and Covenants, the Lord defines truth for us: "Truth is knowledge of things as they are, and as they were, and as they are to come" (93:24). As we ponder this definition, it becomes clear that the truth in a telestial world includes some things that aren't truth in a celestial world. Think about the things that really *are* in this telestial world. The truth is that in a telestial world there are thieves and terrorists and earthquakes and car accidents and death. Truth in a telestial sphere includes many negative things that will not be part of things "as they are to come." This creates a problem in that we sometimes think of truth only in terms of the eternal gospel truths or celestial truth—we think of truth as synonymous with righteousness and goodness. But if you were called into court to testify as a witness to a car accident, you would tell exactly what you saw happen, not what *should* have happened. When we think about it, we realize that there are eternal, celestial truths that we need to learn and strive to incorporate into our mortal lives, but there are also telestial truths that we need to learn to deal with.

Why is it important to understand this distinction? Because

while we learn about and strive to incorporate the Lord's truth into our lives, we now live in a telestial world and the Spirit prompts us to navigate through our telestial experiences. If our expectations are based upon what *should* happen, we create static and run the risk of missing the promptings the Spirit sends us. Too often, we spend our time fretting over what *should be* instead of dealing with what *is*.

Living in a telestial world means that many things will occur that try and test us. But knowing the Lord's teachings, we want and expect more—especially of others. Let me share a very simple story that will make this clearer. Imagine that you are walking down the hall at Church and see a young man walking toward you. You see his long, straggly hair and your mind immediately fills with thoughts such as, "His hair is too long. He should get a haircut. Why don't his parents take him to the barber?"

While your mind is churning with these negative, judgmental thoughts of what should be, the Spirit is prompting you to smile, greet the young man, and ask him how things are going. But because you are so busy thinking about what *he* should do, you don't hear the prompting as to what *you* should do. In teaching about the Spirit, Henry B. Eyring explained, "I bear you my testimony that the scriptures are not being poetic when they describe the Holy Ghost as the still, small voice. It is so quiet that if you are noisy inside, you won't hear it. It is real" (Henry B. Eyring, *To Draw Closer To God: A Collection of Discourses* [Salt Lake City: Deseret Book Co., 1997], 18).

In a perfect world, perhaps every male would have short, well-groomed hair, but the truth is we don't live in a perfect world. In fact, we don't even know what hairstyles will be like in a perfect world. Hairstyles are a cultural phenomenon. Therefore, this kind of critical thinking does no one any good—not the young man and not the person who is criticizing him. We live in a telestial world, so while we strive to learn and be worthy of celestial truths, we need to deal with telestial truths in such a way that we don't shut out the Spirit.

Let's look at one more situation that isn't as trivial. In a telestial world we encounter serious situations such as sorrow and pain. Most of us will have to deal with the death of a loved one. When this happens, the Spirit will be there to comfort and guide us through the ordeal. But in these situations, we often find ourselves consumed with thoughts about what should have happened instead of accepting and dealing with the truth. We think things like: "She shouldn't have died yet, "She should have lived to an old age," "I should have gone to see her last week," "I should have been there when she died," "I should have seen the warning signs and gotten her to the doctor sooner." Since our minds are so busy with these negative thoughts, we run the risk of not hearing the Spirit as it comforts and guides us to do "all things what we should do" (2 Ne. 32:5).

The truth is that our loved one died. The truth is we didn't see her last week. The truth is we didn't see the warning signs, and the Spirit is trying to comfort and prompt and help us deal with those truths—with what actually is. If we persist in filling our mind and heart with thoughts of "should" or "what if," we create static and frustration and run the risk of missing the comfort and guidance that will help and heal us. While we are seeking the impossible (comfort for the *should haves* and *shouldn't haves* or for what isn't true), the Spirit is sending comfort for what actually is—for what is true.

The irony of this situation is that while the Lord is trying to comfort and help us, we too often determine that He is not there. But He is always there. If we aren't feeling His presence it isn't because He has stopped sending messages of comfort and direction to us. It is because we have either encountered static or tuned Him out.

# Love Thy Neighbor

*This is my commandment, That*
*ye love one another, as I have loved you.*

John 15:12

**Your life will be full of surprises, and you can expect some trials. But you can also expect deliverance. You can know that God will answer your prayers and help you, so you don't need to be afraid of those trials anymore. And as you use your gifts from him to serve others, you can feel his love for them, and you can begin to love them as well.**

Henry B. Eyring, *To Draw Closer to God*, 88–89

When asked by a Pharisee which was the greatest commandment in the law, Jesus answered that the greatest commandment is to love God and the second is to "Love thy neighbour as thyself" (Matt. 22:39). Sometimes that verse is used to teach that we need to love ourselves and that we can't possibly love others unless we love ourselves first. But Jesus was speaking these words to Pharisees who had no problem loving themselves. They were proud and full of a feeling of their own self-worth. His instruction for them was a call to love others as much as they already loved themselves, to care for others as well as they cared for themselves.

Later, when speaking to His disciples, the Savior gave very different instructions. He said, "A new commandment I give unto you, That ye love one another; as I have loved you, that ye also love one another" (John 13:34). As disciples of Christ, our task isn't to concentrate on loving ourselves so we can love others. The Savior instructed, "Whosoever will save his life shall lose it: and whosoever will lose his life for my sake shall find it" (Matt. 16:25). Therefore, our task is to forget about ourselves and love others.

Henry B. Eyring explained some of the added benefits of forgetting about self. He said, "Another way to obtain a soft heart is to make sure you don't focus too much on yourself or your personal problems and struggles. Instead of thinking of yourself primarily as someone who is seeking purification, think of yourself as someone who is trying to find out who around you needs your help. Pray that way and then reach out. When you act under such inspiration, it will have a sanctifying effect on you" (ibid, 110–13).

To me this is good news because it simplifies life. It is so difficult to go through life trying to convince yourself that you are all right—that you are worthwhile and wonderful. Surprisingly, it takes an enormous amount of effort and is a constant battle. But if instead we forget all about ourselves and seek to minister to the needs and wants of others, we wake up one morning to discover that without any concentrated effort we like ourselves. But we can't dwell on the thought too long or we grow prideful.

By definition, *love* is the "unselfish loyal and benevolent concern for the good of another." It is extremely difficult to have "unselfish concern" if we are first trying to love ourselves. And the phrase "for the good of another" implies that love is something turned outward not inward. This selfless love is the great test of discipleship. As Jesus said, "By this shall all men know that ye are my disciples, if ye have love one to another" (John 13:34–35).

The promise is that if we will simplify our lives by forgetting about ourselves, Jesus Christ will remember us. We are to take care of others, and He in turn will take care of us.

# Nurtured by Good

*For behold, after ye have been nourished by*
*the good word of God all the day long,*
*will ye bring forth evil fruit, that ye*
*must be hewn down and cast into the fire?*

Jacob 6:7

**True doctrine, understood, changes attitudes and behavior. The study of the doctrines of the gospel will improve behavior quicker than a study of behavior will improve behavior.**

Boyd K. Packer, "Do Not Fear," *Ensign*, May 2004, 79

---

I was raised in the Church by wonderful parents. My father loved the scriptures, and many a family meal was seasoned by scripture discussions. I grew up listening to stories of Nephi and Alma and all the great Book of Mormon prophets told not from a book but from my father's heart. He especially loved Captain Moroni. Stories from the scriptures were as much a part of our home life as the furniture.

Because of this, I loved the scriptures and read them whenever I had time or was in need, which I thought was often enough. But I had only been married eight years when I found out that "whenever" isn't often enough. At that time, I was called to be on a committee to help write lesson manuals for the Church auxiliaries. I was the youngest person on the six-member committee and very intimidated by the other members, who were extremely accomplished. The committee met weekly at five o'clock in the evening, which meant that the men came directly from work and didn't have time to eat, so sandwiches were provided. During the first few minutes of each meeting, we ate and talked about our week.

Not many weeks into the assignment I realized that one of the reasons these people were so wonderful is that every one of them started his or her day with scripture reading. They didn't just read scriptures once in a while when they had time. It was part of their daily routine just like brushing their teeth or eating breakfast. They never missed, and it wasn't because someone had told them they should do it. They did it because they loved it. They did it because it fed their souls. That was very evident by the way they talked. If time were a problem and they had to leave something out of their day, they would rather leave out brushing their teeth or making their bed or eating their breakfast than give up scripture study! Mind you, none of them told me these things; it was just evident.

But then something else began to occur to me. Week after week as we ate and talked about our lives, I realized that these people didn't just read the scriptures. What they learned each morning was an integral part of their lives! They'd mention problems they were having with their teenage children and how one morning as they were reading scripture the solution to the problems would come to them. They'd tell about caring for older parents and how just at the point of utter discouragement their morning reading buoyed them up and allowed them to serve with charity. Week after week the stories continued, not in a preachy or holier-than-thou way, but with a feeling of gratitude and a matter-of-fact certainty that scripture reading always brought those kind of results.

As I already stated, I loved the scriptures and I knew that the prophets had asked us to study the scriptures daily, but I had four children under the age of seven and somehow figured that exempted me. But as I listened and learned from my fellow committee members, I realized that I was cheating myself. Because of their example, I began to make scripture study a daily priority and to experience the blessings for myself.

In church meetings, I'd heard many stories like this: Someone had a problem they were pondering. Seeking answers, they went to the scriptures and miraculously opened to the very verse that answered their problem. I'd never had that experience. But what I realized as I began to study daily was that it wasn't always the words I was reading that brought the answers. I could be reading about Alma digging trenches and building walls to fortify cities, and somehow the answer would come to me as to what a particular child needed or what decision I needed to make to solve a certain dilemma. I learned that by setting aside time and going to a sacred place (the scriptures), I created time and space for the Spirit to speak to me about what I needed to know and do.

Of course, I learned the scripture stories and the doctrines of the gospel, which has been an enormous blessing in my life, but the greatest blessings came from what was communicated to me "between the lines." The scriptures have lifted me when I was discouraged. They have comforted me when I was in physical pain. They have guided when I could see no way out of a problem. They have increased my joy when I was already happy. They have empowered me to do things I never imagined I could do. In short, I have been nourished by the good word of the good news.

The obvious answer to Jacob's question—"After ye have been nourished by the good word of God all the day long, will ye bring forth evil fruit?"—is "No!" There is no way you can remain in the trenches of evil or darkness or despair if you are constantly nourished by the good word. I've learned that for myself. There is transcendent power in the words of the scriptures. There is comfort, love, peace, and joy in making them part of your daily life.

# Attitude

*Counsel with the Lord in all thy doings, and he will direct thee for good; yea, when thou liest down at night lie down unto the Lord, that he may watch over you in your sleep; and when thou risest in the morning let thy heart be full of thanks unto God; and if ye do these things, ye shall be lifted up at the last day.*

Alma 37:37

**Certainly one of our God-given privileges is the right to choose what our attitude will be in any given set of circumstances. We can let the events that surround us determine our actions—or we can personally take charge and rule our lives, using as guidelines the principles of pure religion.**

Marvin J. Ashton, "Pure Religion," *Ensign*, Nov. 1982, 63

The striking thing for me about Alma 37:37 is the way it summarizes the simplicity of the gospel of Jesus Christ. In just one verse, we are directed to do three things: (1) counsel with the Lord; (2) at night, lie down unto the Lord; and (3) each morning, be filled with gratitude. If we do these things, we are promised that (1) God will direct us for good, (2) He will watch over us, and (3) He will lift us up at the last day. As always, what He gives us is far greater than what He asks of us.

At first glance, these admonitions seem to be about prayer,

submitting to the Lord, and giving thanks to Him. But one day I realized that there was a common thread that tied all three together. All pertain to attitude—the attitude of putting God first in our lives. By counseling with Him, submitting to Him, and constantly thanking Him, we make Him an integral part of our daily lives: part of our thinking, our very foundation. In other words, as we regularly do these things, our basic attitudes will be different than the attitudes of the natural man. We will look at life differently.

The word *attitude* means "a deliberately adopted, or habitual, mode of regarding the object of thought" (John Ayto, *Dictionary of Word Origins* [New York: Arcade, 1990], 259). The concept this word derived from originally applied to the design arts and had to do with position and stance of objects. The original term used to convey this idea was the word *aptitude,* but that word came to mean "inclination or tendency" or "a natural talent." Eventually, the word *aptitude* evolved into the word *attitude* and came to mean not just a physical position, but a mental position. *Attitude* now refers to a way of thinking about things. It is the mental "stance" a person assumes.

With this understanding, I imagine attitude as a pair of eyeglasses that I view the world through. Depending on whether I am looking through the blue attitude lens or the red or the green lens will make a difference in how I interpret what I see. This brings us back to where we started. If our attitudes are determined by our counseling with God, submitting to God, and constantly thanking God, we view life very differently than if our attitudes are about getting ahead in life or being the best or finding the easiest way to do things. Each of us has some underlining attitude that directs our lives—a lens we see through. The important thing is to come to realize what lens we are using.

I find that one of the greatest hindrances to my living the gospel of Jesus Christ and "being directed for good" is that too often my attitudes are determined by habit rather than conscious choice. Growing up, I picked up attitudes from the world around me without realizing I was doing so. But if instead of acting out of habit, I counsel with the Lord, submit myself to Him, and remember His hand in all things, my life goes very differently. The difference is in the attitude.

Am I saying my prayers or am I praying? Am I making my offerings or am I offering? Am I seeking approval or to be approved? Am I saying thanks or am I thankful? Am I going through the temple or letting the temple go through me? These differences in attitude are subtle, but so important.

# The Power of Never

*Because he had fallen from heaven, and had*
*become miserable forever, he sought also the misery of*
*all mankind. Wherefore, he said unto Eve, yea,*
*even that old serpent, who is the devil, who is the father*
*of all lies, wherefore he said: Partake of the forbidden*
*fruit, and ye shall not die, but ye shall be as*
*God, knowing good and evil.*

2 Nephi 2:18

**Because the evil one is ever at work, our vigilance cannot be relaxed—not even for a moment. A small and seemingly innocent invitation can turn into a tall temptation which can lead to tragic transgression. Night and day, at home or away, we must shun sin and hold fast that which is good.**

Russell M. Nelson, "Set in Order Thy House," *Ensign*, Nov. 2001, 69

From the very beginning, the adversary's only goal has been to make us miserable. And he isn't content with making us miserable for a day or an hour. He wants us miserable forever—miserable like he is. Prophets through the ages have warned us how to avoid this misery, but still many of us disregard their teachings. Somehow we think a little sin won't matter, so we flirt with danger.

There are those who like to "try" things out for themselves.

They reason that one drink of alcohol won't hurt. One cigarette won't hurt. Doing something wrong just once won't matter. But when we move from the realms of *never* into the realm of *just-this-once,* we weaken our resolve.

I have a little mind game that helps me with this. If I have never committed a certain sin, I have done it zero times. Therefore, I like to imagine myself standing in the center of a great big 0. All around I am fortified and protected by the walls of the 0. I am sheltered from any lurking dangers outside the walls of that 0. As long as I am inside that 0—saying "never" to the temptations of the adversary—I am safe and secure within its walls. There is power in even the thought "I have never tasted alcohol" or "I have never cheated on my tithing" or "I have never stolen anything."

But as soon as I give in to temptation, I step outside that 0 and onto a one—a very thin, balance-beam-like 1. Perched atop that 1, I have lost my protection. No longer is there anything surrounding me. Nothing protects me. Instead I must navigate that fine line and risk slipping to a 2 or 3 or something else that has no protective walls.

But what if saying *never* is already impossible? In many areas of our lives it is too late to say *never.* We have already slipped so far down the number line that we don't even remember what number we are on. What then?

The good news is that if we recognize how vulnerable we are outside that 0, and desire to return to the safety of that circle, we can repent and be restored to its protection. We can start over! The Hebrew word for repentance, *shoob,* means just that—to return, restore, refresh, or repair. Repentance returns us to the safety and security and shelter of the Lord. And the 0 symbolically represents that place of safety and security. If we can see ourselves fortified in the center of that 0 and relish the thought that since repenting we have never committed the sin, we can be strengthened to endure. Our resolve can be fortified.

When I find myself tempted to sin, or have already done something wrong, I close my eyes and imagine myself in the circumscribed safety of the 0. I savor the feel and the comfort of being snuggled in those protective boundaries. I study my scripture more intently. I pray more fervently, and I focus more on taking the sacrament worthily. Thus I put myself back in the safety of *never.*

# Restoration

*[God] hath given unto you that ye might*
*know good from evil, and he hath given unto you that*
*ye might choose life or death; and ye can do good and be*
*restored unto that which is good, or have that which*
*is good restored unto you; or ye can do evil, and have*
*that which is evil restored unto you.*

Helaman 14:31

**The assurance of resurrection also gives us a powerful incentive to keep the commandments of God during our mortal lives. Resurrection is much more than merely reuniting a spirit to a body held captive by the grave. We know from the Book of Mormon that the resurrection is a restoration that brings back "carnal for carnal" and "good for that which is good" (Alma 41:13).**

Dallin H. Oaks, "Resurrection," *Ensign*, May 2000, 14

I used to envision the Final Judgment as a day in court. According to that perception, I would go before the Eternal Judge and He would recount all the events of my life and then assign me to a kingdom according to how many good or bad deeds I had done. I even imagined a scale with good deeds on one side and bad on the other and me standing by anxiously hoping the good tipped the scale. After determining my judgment, the Eternal Judge would pronounce my fate, wave His hand, and

I would be suddenly transformed into a telestial, terrestrial, or celestial being and waved on to my eternal abode.

Now I have a very different vision of Judgment Day. It was the word *restored* found in the scripture from Helaman that began this chapter that changed my perception. I now believe that as soon as I'm resurrected I'll know whether I'm a telestial, terrestrial, or celestial being, and the Judgment spoken of in the scriptures will be more of an accounting. I now envision it more like a temple recommend interview. When I enter the bishop's office, I know whether I am worthy or not. The bishop doesn't pronounce judgment. Instead he asks several questions and I make an accounting of my own obedience. I declare whether I am worthy or not. He doesn't. The difference is that at the Final Judgment, a person will not lie to the Lord.

In D&C 88:27–31, we find an explanation of this restoration. There we are told that those who responded to celestial glory while on earth will be restored to their celestial bodies, those who responded to terrestrial glory will be restored to their terrestrial bodies, and those who responded to telestial glory will be restored to their telestial bodies. In other words, every moment of every day we are responding to influences or to a "glory by which [our] bodies are quickened." We were given a telestial body at birth, but if we respond to terrestrial or celestial influences and live by terrestrial or celestial laws, our bodies are literally changed into terrestrial or celestial bodies.

Elder Bruce R. McConkie explained it this way, "By one degree of obedience or another, all men, in this life, develop either celestial, terrestrial, or telestial bodies (or in the case of those destined to be sons of perdition, bodies of a baser sort). In the resurrection all men receive back again 'the same body which was a natural body,' whether it be celestial, terrestrial, or what have you. That body is then quickened by the glory attending its particular type, and the person receiving the body then goes automatically, as it were, to the kingdom of glory where that degree of glory is found" (Bruce R. McConkie, *Doctrinal New Testament Commentary*, 3 vols. [Salt Lake City: Bookcraft, 1965], 1:196).

When we realize that every moment of every day we are changing our physical bodies one decision at a time, we live life differently. Just stopping to ask yourself, "Is this a celestial, terrestrial, or telestial response?" can help us make better decisions. It also helps us understand why excuses and rationalizations are so detrimental. Yes, we can think, "Everyone else is doing it," or, "It won't hurt just this once," or, "It's just a little thing." But if we think like that, we will be restored to the glory that generates that kind of thinking, and no celestial being thinks like that.

If we want to be restored to a celestial body, we need to develop a celestial mind, and the way to do that is to make celestial decisions.

# The Power to Be Good

*Yea, we believe all the words which
thou hast spoken unto us; and also, we know of their
surety and truth, because of the Spirit of the Lord
Omnipotent, which has wrought a mighty change in us,
or in our hearts, that we have no more disposition
to do evil, but to do good continually.*

Mosiah 5:2

**Accountability is the natural product of agency and is the basis of the plan of life. We are responsible for our own actions and accountable to God for what we choose to do with our lives. Life is God's gift to us, and what we do with it is our gift to him.**

Elaine Cannon, "Agency and Accountability," *Ensign,* Nov. 1983, 88

---

Many years ago, while working on an article that was to be published, I sat through a long meeting with my editor, trying to resolve changes he wanted in the manuscript. The basic thesis of the article was that God has given us agency so that we can choose between good and evil and become like Him. The undergirding point throughout was that the choice is ours. In very subtle ways and much to my dismay, however, the editor had added and changed words so that the meaning of the article was distorted. Instead of conveying the idea that through agency we decide who we will become, the article now portrayed people as victims of circumstances that determine what they do and are. This was the opposite of what I intended, but I struggled to make the editor understand what was wrong. The meeting was cordial, but every time I questioned the changes and pointed out how they modified the meaning, he defended his changes and refused to go back to the original intent.

Finally, in response to one of his arguments I said, "But because of agency we can change." He looked at me intently and answered, "No, we can't. I have a very bad temper, and the reason I have a short fuse is that when I was five years old I was scalded with hot water in a kitchen accident. Ever since, I've had this bad temper, and there is absolutely nothing I can do about it."

I've pondered that conversation over and over and wondered how many of my own faults I've dismissed in such a way. It is tempting to use life's adverse experiences as an excuse. But it is not truth. The truth is that any action, reaction, or response is a choice—even if we have been doing it so long it is now habitual. And while it is easy to place blame and attempt to escape responsibility for our faults, it will never bring us happiness. When I deny the great gift of agency that has been given me, I may temporarily ease my conscience, but I also stop my progress.

The first step to using our agency is to acknowledge that we have the power to change. In any moment we have the power to choose good, but without first acknowledging that we can change, we never will. That doesn't mean change will be easy, but it does give us great hope. We don't have to be miserable. If we go around thinking that we are the way we are because of our parents, or because of past experience, or because of adverse conditions, we are burdened by the thought that our life can't change unless others change or circumstances change. Once we recognize that agency gives us the power to change our faults or attitudes, we can take steps to overcome them. We are in control!

I've often hurt for my friend who thought his short fuse could not be rectified. How terrible it would be to go through life thinking that because of an incident in our youth we have to live our life lashing out and hurting the people we love, and that there is absolutely nothing we can do about it. The good news of the gospel is that we *can* do something about it. We can change. We can grow. We can choose to be different because God has given us the ability to choose good over evil.

# Holding Fast

*O Lord, I have trusted in thee, and I will trust
in thee forever. I will not put my trust in the arm of
flesh; for I know that cursed is he that putteth his trust
in the arm of flesh. Yea, cursed is he that putteth his
trust in man or maketh flesh his arm.*

2 Nephi 4:34

**Are you and I daily reading, studying, and searching the
scriptures in a way that enables us to hold fast to the rod
of iron—or are you and I merely clinging? Are you and I
pressing forward toward the fountain of living waters—
relying upon the word of God? These are important
questions for each of us to ponder prayerfully.**

David A. Bednar, CES Fireside for Young Adults, 4 Feb. 2007,
Brigham Young University

---

The gospel of Jesus Christ is meant to be enjoyable—to bring happiness. But sometimes we get so uptight about living the gospel and doing what is right that we choke the joy right out of it. That is as dangerous as not living the gospel, and it usually leads to the same consequences.

In Lehi's dream, he sees five groups of people. The people in the first group (see 1 Ne. 8:21–23) are moving forward trying to find the path that will take them to the tree of life. They find the path and begin to travel it, but as the mists of darkness encompass them, they lose their way. They get lost in the temptations of life.

People in the second group (see 1 Ne. 8:24) also move forward until they catch hold of the rod of iron, but they survive the mists of darkness by clinging to the rod of iron. Eventually, they make it to the tree and partake of the fruit, but after tasting the fruit, they look across the gulf of filthy waters and see a beautiful and spacious building that hovers over the ground on the other side of the river. The people in the building are mocking the people who are partaking of the fruit. Giving heed to the people in the building, the partakers become ashamed and fall back into the mists of darkness.

The people in the great and spacious building (1 Ne. 8:26) are the third group. These are the people the world deems successful—the rich and the famous. There are athletes, movie stars, intelligentsia, politicians, etc., who have made a name for themselves in the world while disdaining God and the ways of righteousness. They take great delight in the pleasures of the world and tout them to others. When Nephi sees this same vision, he explains that the building is the "vain imaginations and the pride of the children of men" (1 Ne. 11:18).

People in the fourth group (1 Ne. 8:30) also take hold of the rod of iron, and like the second group they press forward. However, the description of how this group holds onto the rod is different. Instead of "clinging" to the rod, this group traverses the path by "continually holding fast to the rod of iron." When they eventually reach the tree, they fall down in humility and partake of the fruit.

No one in the last group (1 Ne. 8:31) even attempts to make it to the tree. These people have their hearts set on the people in the building. They wander in the fields and through the mists in an attempt to find their way to the foundation-less building.

For this reason, I've always thought of them as the "great-and-spacious-building wannabes." They aren't famous or recognized by the world, but they want to be the rich and famous and so they imitate them. They dress like them, drive the same cars, and seek after the same pleasures. They study what the people in the building do, and in any way they can, they imitate, mimic, and worship them.

Studying the groups is informative, but the most interesting comparison for me is between groups 2 and 4. It seems to me that Nephi is conveying something very subtle in the contrasts between these two groups. While both groups partake of the fruit, there are two major differences in the way they go about it that give us clues as to why one group remains faithful and the other falls away. When group 2 reaches the tree, they taste the fruit and immediately look out beyond the tree. Perhaps they are looking to see if anyone has noticed the great thing they have done, or they look to the world expecting approval, applause, or praise. When they discover that instead of being cheered they are jeered, they are disappointed.

Pondering why this group failed reminds me of something Elder Neal A. Maxwell once said, "By paying more attention to what we are rather than exclusively to what we do, our public and our private persons will be the same—the man or the woman of Christ. Our intrinsic value is not dependent upon mortal acclaim anyway; in fact, the world may actually see us as weak and foolish (see 1 Cor. 1:27). Countering, however, are divine affirmations, including this one: 'The Spirit itself beareth witness with our spirit, that we are the children of God' (Rom. 8:16) (Neal A. Maxwell, "The Tugs and Pulls of the World, *Ensign*, Nov. 2000, 35).

Unlike group 2, group 4 must have been in tune with these "divine affirmations." When they reach the tree, they fall down. Nephi doesn't explain, but it seems to be a worshipful act expressing both humility and rejoicing. They have arrived at their destination and are no longer searching. Instead they bow in gratitude and love. The journey has been worthwhile. The fruit is good. The people need no outside approval; they are happy.

But even more interesting is the difference in the way the two groups move along the rod of iron. One group clings, the other holds fast. The definition of *cling* is "to adhere to something, as by grasping, sticking, embracing, or entwining." The phrase *hold fast* is defined as "to maintain a grasp or grip on something." At first it may seem that these two terms are synonymous, but there are subtle differences.

The word *cling* has negative connotations that are not associated with the term *hold fast.* We speak of a young girl who is over-possessive of her boyfriend as a "clinging vine," and we describe young children who won't let their mother out of their sight as "clinging to her apron strings." In these cases, the word takes on a fearful connotation that includes a sense of desperation and insecurity. This is the point I think Nephi is trying to make. Even though the people in group 2 cling to the rod and make it to the tree, they aren't confident in the word of God, and they don't trust in Jesus Christ. They seem to cling with a sense of desperation as if they think they have to do it all by themselves, as if they are distressed by the endeavor. Because of this, they traverse the path fearfully instead of faithfully. They are doing it by sheer willpower—by themselves.

There can be grave danger in clinging to something. In his

book *The Snow Leopard*, Peter Matthiessen describes the hazards of mountain climbing. He explains that the climber is dependent upon the rope for safety and for leading him to his destination, and that clinging is one of the great dangers a climber must beware of. "It is this clinging, the tightness of panic, that gets people killed: 'to clutch,' in ancient Egyptian, 'to clutch the mountain,' in Assyrian, were euphemisms that signified 'to die'" (Peter Matthiessen, *The Snow Leopard* [New York: Viking Press, 1978], 129–30; see also Mircea Eliade, *Images and Symbols: Studies in Religious Symbolism* [New York: Sheed & Ward, 1961]).

To me Nephi's vision teaches that if we vacillate between the touted pleasures of the world and the word of God, the journey will be miserable and we will eventually lose our grip and become lost in the mist. If we cling to the iron rod, desperately depending on our own strength, we will be miserable. We might make it to the tree, but even if we do, pride will make the fruit taste bitter.

However, if we confidently hold fast to the iron rod, knowing and trusting in the promises of assistance from Jesus Christ, we can relax, enjoy the journey, and have the strength to make it to the end. As Elder Joseph B. Wirthlin stated, "Those who walk in faith will feel their lives encompassed with the light and blessings of heaven. They will understand and know things that others cannot" (Joseph B. Wirthlin, "Shall He Find Faith on the Earth?" *Ensign*, Nov. 2002, 84).

# Harvesting Peaches

*For thou, Lord, art good, and ready*
*to forgive; and plenteous in mercy unto all*
*them that call upon thee.*

Psalms 86:5

**I think [forgiveness] may be the greatest virtue on earth, and certainly the most needed. There is so much of meanness and abuse, of intolerance and hatred. There is so great a need for repentance and forgiveness. It is the great principle emphasized in all of scripture, both ancient and modern. Somehow forgiveness, with love and tolerance, accomplishes miracles that can happen in no other way.**

Gordon B. Hinckley, "Forgiveness," *Ensign*, Nov. 2005, 81

During a late summer storm several years ago, a large limb on one of our peach trees cracked. Heavy with unripened fruit, the limb hung from the tree, looking as if it would break off completely. Not knowing quite what to do, we struggled to keep the limb alive. First my husband braced the damaged limb with a two-by-four to keep it from breaking more. Then he tightly wrapped the cracked portion of the limb to hold it together. Every day we checked my husband's "first-aid" endeavors, and to our surprise the fruit continued to ripen and we reaped a delicious harvest of peaches.

Years later, the image of that peach tree with the two-by-four supporting the damaged limb came back to me as I prepared a lesson on forgiveness. Obviously, the English word *forgive* is made up of two words: the prefix *for* and the verb *give*. When added to a verb, *for* means "away" or "off." *Give* means to "confer, grant, or bestow." Therefore, *forgive* means to cast away what should have been bestowed. So when we ask the Lord to forgive us, we are acknowledging that there is some consequence or punishment due us that we want him to cast away. When we ask others to forgive us, we are asking them to cast away the bad feelings and the consequences that would normally occur from what we have done. And when we forgive others, we are to cast away the negative feelings and give up the idea of exacting any payment or vengeance or retaliation for what has occurred.

Understanding the two words that make up the English word for the concept of forgiveness helped me better comprehend the concept of forgiveness. But it was looking up the Hebrew word that brought back to mind the image of our peach tree with one two-by-four supporting a broken, heavily laden limb. The Hebrew word *nawsaw* centers on the idea of lifting or bearing up or sustaining something. I like that thought. When we forgive others for wronging or hurting us, we, like the two-by-four under my peach tree limb, are actually helping to sustain, support, and bear the other person up. As Elder Neal A. Maxwell once said, "We cannot repent for someone else. But we can forgive someone else, refusing to hold hostage those whom the Lord seeks to set free!" (Neal A. Maxwell, "Repentance," *Ensign*, Nov. 1991, 30).

Forgiving is a way of loving and serving others. By forgiving others who hurt or offend us, we assist and sustain them in their journey back to God just as if we were giving them a hand-up on a steep mountain. Likewise, when others forgive us of our wrongdoings, they support, sustain, and assist us.

But that isn't all. By forgiving others, we put ourselves in a position where the Lord can forgive us. As He explains in D&C 82:1, "Inasmuch as you have forgiven one another your trespasses, even so I, the Lord, forgive you." This doesn't mean that we purchase the Lord's forgiveness by forgiving others, but rather that until we forgive, we are not worthy for Him to forgive us.

When the Lord forgives us, the image of the peach tree changes. The two-by-four holding up a broken limb disappears. When it is the Lord doing the forgiving, the broken limb is not mended but restored to the state of wholeness and health it had before the storm. The image that captures the significance of the Lord's forgiving us is a fruitful limb on a healthy tree with no trace of the crack that once threatened the life of the tree. The Lord sustains and assists us not by propping us up or wrapping our broken limbs, but by healing us so there is actually no more wound. We are made whole again. Thus to forgive others is to be good, but to be forgiven by the Lord is to be all better.

# God's Righteousness

*[God] inviteth them all to come unto him and
partake of his goodness; and he denieth none that come
unto him, black and white, bond and free, male and
female; and he remembereth the heathen; and all are
alike unto God, both Jew and Gentile.*

2 Nephi 26:33

**Never assume that you can make it alone. You need the
help of the Lord. Never hesitate to get on your knees
in some private place and speak with Him. What a
marvelous and wonderful thing is prayer.**

Gordon B. Hinckley, "Stay on the High Road," *Ensign,* May 2004, 114

---

Often the adversary works in very subtle ways to convince us that we will never be good enough, or that the way back to God is so difficult that we might as well give up and enjoy life's pleasures while we can. These are half-truths, which Satan is skilled at inventing and employing. Yes, it is true that on our own we will never be good enough, and that on our own the way is not only difficult but absolutely impossible. But the good news is that we are not on our own.

As Moroni explains, "Come unto Christ, and be perfected *in him,* and deny yourselves of all ungodliness; and if ye shall deny yourselves of all ungodliness, and love God with all your might, mind and strength, then is *his grace sufficient for you, that by his grace ye may be perfect in Christ;* and if by the grace of God ye are perfect in Christ, ye can in nowise deny the power of God. And again, if ye by the grace of God are perfect in Christ, and deny not his power, then are ye sanctified in Christ *by the grace of God,* through the shedding of the blood of Christ, which is in the covenant of the Father unto the remission of your sins, that ye become holy, without spot" (Moroni 10:32–33; emphasis added).

It is easy to read this and think that it pertains to the future—to some distant end of the perfection process when suddenly the grace of God will change things. Sometimes we think we have to go through many years of denying ourselves "all ungodliness" and then when we have proved ourselves Christ will step in to reward and heal us. But when we understand what Moroni is telling us, we realize that it is about healing, helping, and nurturing—on a daily basis. In each moment as we choose what is good, we receive God's grace. Moroni's advice is about making the Lord part of our lives right now. It is about withstanding the constant distractions and temptations of the adversary. It is about allowing God's goodness and grace to encourage and uplift our daily lives instead of letting discouragement and dismay sink us into despair.

God never has, nor will He ever, put any of us in a situation we cannot handle and grow from. How can I make such a statement? Not because I know that you and I are so incredibly capable, or that we are so mighty or strong that we can handle anything and everything life throws at us. I can make that statement because I know that Jesus Christ is marvelously capable. He is mighty and powerful, and He has offered to yoke Himself with anyone willing to be yoked, so that He can help pull the heavy load of life's daily burdens. And from my own experience, I know that He pulls much more than His share.

Most of our problems occur because we let the hustle and bustle of life erase from our minds the fact that God is there, willing to help us pull the load. Elder David B. Haight advised, "Don't be discouraged at seemingly overwhelming odds in your desire to live and to help others live God's commandments. At times it may seem like David trying to fight Goliath. But remember, David did win" (David B. Haight, "Young Women—Real Guardians," *Ensign*, Nov. 1977, 56). And why did David defeat Goliath? Because the Lord helped him, just like He will help us. But instead of remembering this, we try to do it all ourselves. We can't! From the basics of the daily grind to the majestic end of salvation, we are dependent upon the goodness of God.

In the Book of Mormon, Lehi says to his son Jacob, "I know that thou art redeemed, because . . ." and as a reader you expect the rest of that sentence to be about how good and obedient Jacob has been. Instead, Lehi tells Jacob he is saved "because of the righteousness of thy Redeemer" (2 Ne. 2:3). That was true for Jacob, and it is true for us.

Because of this truth, when the adversary tempts me with depressing thoughts that I'm not good enough or that the gospel path is much too difficult, I simply respond, "You're right! I'm not good enough, but Jesus Christ is and He has promised to make me good enough. So leave me alone."

God is good, and He has invited us to partake of that goodness. We do that by surrounding ourselves with good and by trying our best to do good. But in the end it is His goodness that will strengthen, comfort, and save us. It is a mistake to think of that only in the eternal sense. God knows where we are now and what we need now. He will save us daily if we will let Him.

# Tending the Vineyard

*Therefore, he giveth this promise unto you,*
*with an immutable covenant that they shall be fulfilled;*
*and all things wherewith you have been afflicted*
*shall work together for your good, and to my*
*name's glory, saith the Lord.*

Doctrine and Covenants 98:3

**There is a divine purpose in the adversities we encounter every day. They prepare, they purge, they purify, and thus they bless.**

James E. Faust, "The Refiner's Fire," *Ensign,* May 1979, 53

On a macro level, Jacob's allegory of the olive vineyard (see Jacob 5) is a beautiful account of the dispensations of time and how patiently God has worked to nurture and preserve His people. However, when we look at the allegory on a micro level, we learn some very helpful things about how the Lord works with us as individuals. On both levels, the Master of the vineyard is Jesus Christ, and the servants of the vineyard are the prophets and others who teach and serve the Master.

On the micro level, the olive trees represents us as individuals rather than groups of people throughout the history of the world. With this in mind, we see new meaning in the Lord's words: "What could I have done more in my vineyard? Have I slackened mine hand, that I have not nourished it? Nay, I have nourished it, and I have digged about it, and I have pruned it, and I have dunged it; and I have stretched forth mine hand almost all the day long" (Jacob 5:47). Indeed the Lord nourishes us, and His hand is forever stretched forth beckoning us to draw closer to him. He loves us and cares for us constantly, but sometimes we don't recognize His hand in our lives. Sometimes we even pull away from Him or turn against Him in the very moments He is trying to nurture us, but nurturing isn't always pleasant. As Elder Russell M. Nelson informs us, "With celestial sight, trials impossible to change become possible to endure" (Russell M. Nelson, "With God Nothing Shall Be Impossible," *Ensign*, May 1988, 35).

To understand this better, look at the three ways the Lord of the vineyard nurtures His trees. He has His servants dig around them, dung them, and prune them. With our modern chemicals many of us have forgotten just how smelly the job of fertilizing trees can be. Heaping dung around the trees was not a pleasant process, but it was a necessary process in order to get proper nutrition to the trees so that they would produce the best possible fruit.

Likewise, many of us don't realize why a fruit tree is pruned. We think about ridding the tree of dead branches and thinning out crowded branches so that the available nutrients can be concentrated on the remaining branches. But there is one more reason for pruning. When you prune a tree, you cut the top branches off the tree so that light can reach down to all the branches.

Likewise there are several reasons for digging around a tree. When we read about digging, we usually assume the servants are weeding around the tree, aerating the soil, or just loosening the soil. But there is something more going on here. When a person digs in the ground around a tree, surface roots are cut, stressing the tree. This stressing forces sap to flow and actually invigorates the tree.

A friend who has a small orchard once told me about one of his peach trees that refused to give fruit. He was going to cut it down but decided to check with the local nursery first. A nursery employee instructed him to take a piece of rubber garden hose about four feet long and beat the tree. It sounded strange, but he did it, and the next year he had a bumper crop of beautiful peaches. Why? The horticulturist told him that beating does the same thing as digging: it causes the sap to flow to protect the stressed areas, and subsequently the whole tree does better. To me this is similar to the flight-or-fight syndrome in people. When something scares us, the adrenaline flows to give us the extra power and energy we need to meet the crisis.

When we stop to analyze it, none of these processes are pleasant. Being dunged, pruned, or stressed can be painful— and odorous. But sometimes we need to be humbled or stressed. At other times, there may simply be something we need to learn in order to progress. Sometimes a loving God needs to allow us to be traumatized in order to teach us or to change the direction we are going and put us back on course. As Elder Dallin H. Oaks counseled, "When we give thanks in all things, we see hardships and adversities in the context of the purpose of life . . . We are meant to learn and grow through opposition, through meeting our challenges, and through teaching others to do the same . . . the Lord will not only consecrate our afflictions for our gain, but He will use them to bless the lives of countless others" (Oaks, "Thanks," 95).

Think about it. Imagine you have cancer. It is growing but has not spread. Your doctor tells you that an operation to remove the cancer will save your life, but then he says, "An operation will be very traumatic and cause you a lot of pain. It might also have serious complications. I don't want to hurt you, so I couldn't possibly perform the operation."

No one wants a physician like that, and no one wants a God like that. When we feel the pains of life, instead of getting angry and turning away from Him, we need to trust that God knows what He is doing. He loves us and would not cause us pain unless that pain was absolutely necessary in order for us to become like Him.

# The Observatory

*Those that be planted in the house of
the Lord shall flourish in the courts of our God.*

Psalms 92:13

**I believe that the busy person on the farm, in the shop, in the office, or in the household, who has his worries and troubles, can solve his problems better and more quickly in the house of the Lord than anywhere else. If he will . . . [do] the temple work for himself and for his dead, he will confer a mighty blessing upon those who have gone before, and . . . a blessing will come to him, for at the most unexpected moments, in or out of the temple will come to him, as a revelation, the solution of the problems that vex his life. That is the gift that comes to those who enter the temple properly.**

John A. Widstoe, "Temple Worship," *The Utah Genealogical
and Historical Magazine*, Apr. 1921, 63–64

---

When my daughter Laresa lived in Texas, she was running errands one day with her five-year-old son Nate. The last errand on her list was to go to the Church Distribution Center located in the temple. As they hurried from one place to the next, Laresa kept talking to Nate about the temple and telling him that they were going to go there. Finally, she finished the other errands, drove to the temple, purchased her clothing, and started to leave. But Nate would not move. Laresa urged. He didn't move. She bribed. He still didn't move. And since she was in a hurry, she finally demanded. But Nate still refused to move. Finally, in exasperation Laresa knelt beside Nate and asked, "Nate, why won't you come?" Looking intently into his mother's eyes, Nate replied, "Because I haven't seen Jesus yet."

Since my daughter told me this story, I've thought of it almost every time I've gone to the temple. It helps remind me of why I am there. It also reminds me of the dedicatory prayer of the Kirtland Temple. In that prayer, Joseph Smith recounted to God the sacrifice that had gone into building the temple and the price that the people had paid to build a house so that "the Son of Man might have a place to manifest himself to his people" (D&C 109:5). While we probably won't physically see the Savior in the temple, there are many ways He manifests himself to us when we worshipfully attend the temple.

Years ago, I found two great definitions of the word *temple*. The first is "a place set aside by a prophet for observation." The second is "a place where one gets one's bearings on the universe." I have come to know how aptly these definitions describe our temples.

One of the great blessings of the temple is the endowment from our Father in Heaven. The word *endowment* means "to equip or supply with a talent or quality" and is made up of three parts. *En-* is a prefix meaning "to put into or onto." The root of the word *endowment* is *dower,* which comes from the Old French word *douer,* meaning "to provide with a dowry." Clearly, this is the same root word we get our English word *dowry* from. The suffix *-ment* means "process of." So when we put all three parts together, we understand that at its roots, the word *endowment* refers to the process of providing a dowry.

This root meaning is intensified when we remember that throughout the scriptures Jesus Christ proclaims Himself the groom and His covenant people the bride. Thus, symbolically, the endowment is the dowry given to the bride. And what a valuable gift it is! When you do your temple work, President Ezra Taft Benson declared, "You will receive the key of the knowledge of God (see D&C 84:19). You will learn how you can be like Him. Even the power of godliness will be manifest to you (see D&C 84:20). You will be doing a great service to those who have passed to the other side of the veil in order that they might be 'judged according to men in the flesh, but live according to God in the spirit' (D&C 138:34; 1 Peter 4:6). Such are the blessings of the temple and the blessings of frequently attending the temple" (Ezra Taft Benson, "What I Hope You Will Teach Your Children about the Temple," *Ensign*, Aug. 1985, 10).

Indeed, when we worship in the house of the Lord, for those hours we are removed from the busy, hectic pace of the world, and we are allowed to observe life from a clearer perspective.

# Life's GPS

*I know the thoughts that I think toward you,*
*saith the Lord, thoughts of peace, and not*
*of evil, to give you an expected end.*

Jeremiah 29:11

**When you listen for the words of God and follow them, you will hear more. When you do not listen or do not follow, you will hear less and less until finally you may not hear at all.**

Henry B. Eyring, *To Draw Closer to God*, 38

My son purchased a car with a Global Positioning System (GPS) unit. When he first took me for a ride, he programmed in the address of our daughter's house and we followed the pleasant female voice as she gave instructions. A short way before a turn she'd tell us to prepare to turn left in one hundred feet, and as we approached the corner she'd instruct us, "Make a left-hand turn at the next corner." At one point, we purposely took a wrong turn, and she told us to make a U-turn as soon as it was safe and to return to our programmed route. I listened in amazement as the voice guided us to our destination, keeping us exactly on course. But that wasn't all. As we drove, I watched a little arrow on the map turn or move forward as we turned or moved forward. Something out there knew exactly where I was and exactly how to get me to where I was going! To someone who is technologically challenged, it was incredible.

One of the great realizations of my life came when I acknowledged the fact that like the global positioning system, God knows where I am and how to get me where I want to go. In addition, He has given me the gift of His Spirit to guide me back to my heavenly home. Like my son in his car, I need to listen to the directions and follow them. But with God, there is something more. Not only does He know my position, He knows the exact situation I am dealing with and my attitude and feelings and thoughts about the situation. As President Thomas S. Monson explained, "Life's journey is not traveled on a freeway devoid of obstacles, pitfalls, and snares. Rather, it is a pathway marked by forks and turnings. Decisions are constantly before us" (Thomas S. Monson, "The Call for Courage," *Ensign*, May 2004, 54).

To make these decisions, we need the guidance of the Holy Spirit, and as President Monson went on to say in that same General Conference address, the courage to *follow* the Spirit. That courage comes as we trust in God. He knows if I am hurting or excited or sorrowful. He knows if I am being abused or if I am disheartened or challenged or tempted. But the fact that He knows isn't the most important point to acknowledge. Because God loves me, He cannot know what is happening to me without helping me. At all times He is there offering what I need. It is up to me to accept that or reject it.

But there is even more! One of my favorite verses of scripture is the one we started with from Jeremiah 29:11. The King James version is good, but the New Revised Standard Version says it more succinctly. It reads, "Surely I know the plans I have for you, says the Lord, plans for your welfare and not for harm, to give you a future with hope." Not only does God know our position and what we are going through right now, He knows where He is taking us. Therefore, He knows the best way to get us through the present difficulty and on to our future of hope.

When we acknowledge these things, we realize that, instead of becoming discouraged and disheartened at the daily trials and vicissitudes of life—instead of giving in or giving up—we need to look for (and listen for) the guidance He is offering. It is always there. His voice is calling to us, beckoning us to trust in Him, to make a U-turn and return to the right path, to turn left at the upcoming intersection, to take the next freeway exit, or to stay on the road for another forty miles.

His system is much better than a Global Positioning System. It is our eternal GGS: God's Guidance System.

# The Blessings of Heaven

*Ye shall offer for a sacrifice unto me a broken heart
and a contrite spirit. And whoso cometh unto me
with a broken heart and a contrite spirit, him will I
baptize with fire and with the Holy Ghost.*

3 Nephi 9:20

**When we sincerely accept God as our Father and make Him the center of our being, we become conscious of a new aim in life. No longer is the chief end of daily life merely to nourish and to pamper the body as all animals do. Spiritual attainment, not physical indulgence, becomes the chief goal. God is not viewed from the standpoint of what we may get from Him, but what we may give to Him.**

David O. McKay, *Pathways to Happiness* [Salt Lake City: Deseret Book Co., 1966], 198

I used to have a difficult time understanding the difference between the law of sacrifice and the law of consecration. To me they were both about giving up whatever we were called upon to give. The only thing I could detect that made them different is that the law of consecration includes the United Order when it is functioning. But for most of the world's history the United Order hasn't been fully operative. So why two laws?

I began to see a difference when I looked up the words. The Merrian-Webster Online Dictionary says that *sacrifice* is the "surrender of something for the sake of something else," while the word *consecrate* means "to make or declare sacred." The Latin roots of the word *sacrifice* are *sacer*, which means "sacred," and *facere*, which means "to make." So the root meaning of *sacrifice* is "to make sacred." The Latin roots of the word *consecrate* are *com-*, which means "with, together, or thoroughly," and *sacer*, from which the word *sacrifice* comes. Thus, the root meaning of *consecrate* is "with sacredness" or "thoroughly sacred."

The two concepts have similar meanings—both words have to do with making us holy or sacred—but there seems to be a progression from sacrifice to consecration. Sacrifice seems to precede consecration. I began to see that the journey to holiness was a process that first involved sacrifice and eventually developed into consecration.

That helped, but it wasn't all I needed to know. When we talk about the concept of sacrifice, there is the Sacrifice that is the crux of the whole gospel. That is the sacrifice of Jesus Christ, the Atonement that He performed to save us all. To remember the Atonement, people who lived before it occurred brought animals to the tabernacle or temple to be sacrificed on an altar. After the Atonement occurred, people officially commemorated the occasion by partaking of the sacrament. These were and are the formal occasions that remind us of the great gift that has been given to us, the sacrifice of Jesus Christ that was necessary to satisfy the law of justice.

But there is more to the law of sacrifice for you and me than commemorating it. In order to become like Jesus Christ, we also must sacrifice. In the *Lectures on Faith*, we learn that without sacrifice there can be no faith, and without faith we cannot return to our Heavenly Father (see Joseph Smith, *Lectures on Faith,* 6:7).

While most of us will not be called upon to give our lives as Christ did, we must sacrifice our sins, our selfishness, our pride, and anything else we are called upon to sacrifice. Some of the temporal things we are called upon to sacrifice are a tenth of our income, two meals once a month or whenever we are prompted to fast, and harmful foods and substances such as alcohol, tobacco, tea, and coffee. We also sacrifice our time by serving missions, doing temple work, performing in our Church callings, and studying the gospel.

Sacrifice is a way of saying to God that His ways and His world are more important to us than this telestial world and its ways. Sacrifice is a way of proving that our obedience is sincere and not counterfeit. It is the beginning of the process of becoming holy. It is a way of detaching ourselves, at least partially, from many of the things of the world so that we stand apart.

When we stop to analyze the law of sacrifice before and after the Atonement, we see that the law is about divesting or ridding ourselves of the things that tie us to a mortal world: the things that make us telestial. In Old Testament times they sacrificed the best of their animals and produce—very important items in an agrarian society. Today we sacrifice our time, talents, money, and especially the very attitudes and thought processes that are so much a part of this world. We sacrifice feelings of vengeance, taking offense, envy, selfishness, gluttony, pride, and everything else that is unholy. As we do this we come to a point where we sincerely regret all the bad we have done and thought, and we wish with all our hearts we had been and done better. In the gospel, this is known as having a broken heart and a contrite spirit. In other words, we come to the point where we offer the

Savior our sorrowing, repentant self.

Once we have detached ourselves from the telestial world, we are ready to be part of something better, something holy. Consecration, then, is the process of investing ourselves in the kingdom of God. When we have a broken heart and recognize how much we need a Savior, we do all we can to build His kingdom. Therefore, consecration is a process of attaching ourselves to the things of a celestial world—of God's world. It means investing our time, talents, wealth, and anything else God has given us to establishing Zion here on the earth. And what is Zion? In D&C 97:21, the Lord gives us the answer, "Verily, thus saith the Lord, let Zion rejoice, for this is Zion—THE PURE IN HEART." When we are doing all we can to be pure in heart and to help others to be pure in heart, we are living the law of consecration. We are investing in the kingdom of God.

It is interesting to see how these processes are illustrated in the story of the children of Israel. God miraculously led them out of Egypt, but they were not yet ready to enter the promised land. They had not detached themselves from the ways of Egypt. So, for forty years they wandered in the wilderness. After those people who remembered and clung to the ways of Egypt died, the Lord took them into the promised land, where they were to build Zion. Then they were to invest themselves in the new land and in new ways of being and thinking. They failed in their task, but we can learn from them. We can emotionally detach ourselves from the telestial world (sacrifice), and give our time and energy to building God's kingdom here on earth (consecration). By so doing, we attach ourselves to Zion.

# The Pure Love of Christ

*If ye have not charity, ye are nothing, for*
*charity never faileth. Wherefore, cleave unto charity,*
*which is the greatest of all, for all things must fail—*
*But charity is the pure love of Christ, and it endureth*
*forever; and whoso is found possessed of it at*
*the last day, it shall be well with him.*

Moroni 7:46–47

**Love is one of the chief characteristics of Deity, and ought to be manifested by those who aspire to be the sons of God. A man filled with the love of God, is not content with blessing his family alone, but ranges through the whole world, anxious to bless the whole human race.**

Joseph Smith, *Teachings*, 174

One day during the opening hymn of a Book of Mormon class I was teaching, I looked out over the young faces of my students and felt an overwhelming love surge through me. The feeling didn't surprise me at first, as I've often felt it for my students. Even though I don't usually get to know them very well, the mother in me makes me want to take them under my wing and protect them. I often tell my classes that when they take a course from me they aren't getting another professor, they're getting another mother!

However, that day as I continued to watch my students sing, the feeling grew until it was almost unbearable joy, and I said to myself, "Wow! This love I have for them is so powerful." As I thought that, a voice inside my head said, "No, what you are feeling is *my* love for them."

The class must have thought I'd lost it, because tears began to flow, and I struggled to compose myself in order to begin the day's discussion. The amazing thing is that for the next several hours the world looked brighter. The colors seemed more vivid, and I wanted to hug everyone I encountered. I felt absolutely invincible. I think if someone had asked me to fly, I could have done it. But it wasn't until later as I pondered on what had happened that I realized what I'd felt wasn't an emotion. Before when someone talked about charity or love, I thought in terms of emotions. That's how we usually think about love. But that day I understood that the charity the Lord let me feel for those students was an actual power. It was enabling and uplifting, and it purged everything negative right out of me.

That experience sent me to Moroni 7 to learn more. In that great chapter on faith, hope, and charity, I found something I hadn't seen before. When Mormon speaks of faith, he repeatedly instructs us to have "faith in Christ." When he speaks of hope, he asks what should we "hope for," then answers that we should have "hope through the atonement of Christ, and the power of his resurrection, to be raised unto life eternal" (Moroni 7:41).

The prepositions used here are important. *In* is a function word used to indicate inclusion, location, or position within limits. Thus we understand that faith is something we have that we locate in Christ. We place our trust and belief *in* Him. The preposition *for,* which Mormon uses in his question on hope, indicates the "object or recipient of a perception, desire, or activity." The preposition *through*, which he uses in his answer, means "by way of." Both of these words indicate that hope, like faith, begins in us and we then extend our desire and perceptions to expect that our redemption will come by way of Jesus Christ.

But when Mormon speaks of charity, he defines it as "the pure love of Christ." *Of* means "derived or coming from; caused by; produced by; issuing from." Charity, then, is not something that originates with us. It is not something we generate. Charity resides in God. It is a gift from God. It is a power that God chooses to share with His righteous sons and daughters. That is why "charity never faileth" (Moroni 7:46), because it is His. That is why when we have charity, "we shall be like him" (Moroni 7:48). Elder Jeffrey R. Holland explained this so well when he said, "Only the pure love of Christ will see us through. It is Christ's love which suffereth long, and is kind. It is Christ's love which is not puffed up nor easily provoked. Only his pure love enables him—and us—to bear all things, believe all things, hope all things, and endure all things (see Moroni 7:45)" (Jeffrey R. Holland, "He Loved Them unto the End," *Ensign*, Nov. 1989, 25).

All of us are given experiences from time to time that allow us to feel this love. Usually these experiences come in the form of the "tender mercies of the Lord" (1 Ne. 1:20). These are ordinary experiences that bless our lives and let us know He is watching over us, loving us. Sometimes they are so ordinary that if we aren't careful we don't recognize them as gifts from God. Once in a great while, these experiences are more dramatic, as they were for me that day in the classroom. But they are always given to help us recognize that God's pure love is operating in our lives. And they are always given to encourage us to seek after that power in order to bless the lives of others.

When we realize what an incredible gift charity is—not something we generate, but something given to us—we understand why Mormon exhorts us to petition the Lord for it. "Pray unto the Father *with all the energy of heart*," he says, "that ye may be filled with this love, which he hath bestowed upon all who are true followers of his Son, Jesus Christ" (Moroni 7:48; emphasis added).

# Good in the Midst of Evil

*My son, be faithful in Christ: and may
not the things which I have written grieve thee,
to weigh thee down unto death; but may Christ lift thee
up, and may his sufferings and death, and the showing
his body unto our fathers, and his mercy and long-
suffering, and the hope of his glory and of eternal
life, rest in your mind forever.*

Moroni 9:25

**There are two kinds of faith. One of them functions ordinarily in the life of every soul. It is the kind of faith born by experience; it gives us certainty that a new day will dawn. . . . It is the kind of faith that relates us with confidence to that which is scheduled to happen. . . . There is another kind of faith, rare indeed. This is the kind of faith that causes things to happen. It is the kind of faith that is worthy and prepared and unyielding, and it calls forth things that otherwise would not be. It is the kind of faith that moves people. It is the kind of faith that sometimes moves things. Few men possess it. It comes by gradual growth. It is a marvelous, even a transcendent, power, a power as real and as invisible as electricity. Directed and channeled, it has great effect.**

Boyd K. Packer, "What is Faith?" "Faith" (Salt Lake City: Deseret Book Co., 1983), 42

At the end of the Book of Mormon, Moroni shares with us a letter written to him by his father. In this letter Mormon bares his soul to his son, and since Moroni included it in his plates, to us. We see a man sorrowing over the suffering of his people. His soul is doubly grieved because he knows that if the people would just repent, they could escape the horrific things they are experiencing. Knowing this with all his heart, he explains, "Behold, I am laboring with them continually; and when I speak the word of God with sharpness they tremble and anger against me; and when I use no sharpness they harden their hearts against it; wherefore, I fear lest the Spirit of the Lord hath ceased striving with them" (Moroni 9:4).

Mormon knows that the solution to his people's problems is simple. He laments the fact that they were once a "a civil and a delightsome people" (Moroni 9:12). We feel his deep anguish as he describes the terrible conditions of rape, murder, pillage, hunger, death, and forced cannibalism that exist among the people. We marvel that in the midst of all this horror he gives Moroni the advice not to be "weighed down." But what is more interesting than what Mormon says is what he doesn't say. Despite the horrific conditions, Mormon is not outwardly concerned about Moroni's physical well-being or safety. He doesn't seem concerned about Moroni being killed or wounded. Instead, Mormon is worried about his son being cut off from the Spirit because of all the evil and sin around him.

There are several things we can learn from this. The most obvious is the pain that sin causes. The second is that people in sin are blind to the causes of their problems. Instead, they need a prophet to help them see, but they often do not respond to a prophet. They argue with him and refuse to believe his words.

But one of the more subtle things we can learn from this letter is that even in the midst of extreme depravity it is possible to be righteous. It is possible to be good even when everyone around you is participating in and creating evil. The question we have to ask ourselves is, how can we do that?

Mormon advises Moroni not to let the evil around him grieve him or weigh him down unto death. (see Moroni 9:25). Mormon understands that even in these horrendous conditions if Moroni dwells on the evil around him it will depress and discourage him—it will cause spiritual death as surely as participating in the evil will cause spiritual death. Instead, in the midst of this evil, Mormon advises Moroni to think about Christ and let his hope center in Christ—in other words, to remember Christ at all times.

Mormon is sharing one of the great secrets of life with his son. Despite the horrendous conditions, Moroni can and should push away the negative thoughts and let "the hope of [Christ's] glory and of eternal life, rest in your mind forever" (Moroni 9:25). Hopefully, none of us will witness the level of evil that Mormon and Moroni endured. But all of us will witness evil. It is part of the mortal experience. Therefore, we too need to learn not to let the evil around us weigh us down, but instead we need to lift our sights and carry thoughts of Christ and His Atonement in our hearts. We need to hold fast to the hope of Christ's glory.

There are many ways we can help ourselves to do this. When evil thoughts begin to weigh us down, we can sing or listen to a hymn, recite or read scripture, serve another person, think of a joyous moment with a loved one, imagine standing before the bar of God and feeling of His great love, or anything else that replaces the negative thought with something good. We must remember that "The conflict between good and evil will be fierce but out of every struggle will come the victory of the right and of the truth" (Melvin J. Ballard, *Conference Report*, Oct. 1936, 101–2).

Good has more power than evil and if we choose good in whatever moment we are in, like Mormon and Moroni, we will triumph.

# Be Still and Know

*Therefore, let your hearts be comforted
concerning Zion; for all flesh is in mine hands;
be still and know that I am God.*

Doctrine and Covenants 101:16

**Many of us get so involved in our day-to-day tasks and worldly pursuits that we do not notice the many small miracles that constantly occur around us. This is one reason we may lose contact with the Holy Spirit and lose awareness of His promptings.**

Ronald T. Halverson, "Obeying the Whisperings of the Holy Ghost,"
*Ensign,* Aug. 2007, 56–58

---

Many years ago a close friend of mine took the missionary lessons in our home and eventually became a member of the LDS Church. Years later as I spoke with her about her conversion she said, "Hearing the gospel wasn't like I was being taught anything new. When the missionaries told me something it was like I was remembering it. It was as if those things had been part of me—in my heart—forever and they just had to be moved to my head." At the time I thought the statement interesting, but it came to mean a lot more to me recently.

During the sacrament a while back, I opened my scriptures to D&C 20 and reread the words the priests had just uttered. For some reason the repetition of the concept *remember* hit me harder than usual, and I stopped to reread the phrases the word appeared in again. First, in the prayer on the bread are these words: "That they may eat in remembrance of the body of thy Son, and witness unto thee, O God, the Eternal Father, that they are willing to take upon them the name of thy Son, and always remember him." In the prayer on the water, the words are slightly different: "That they may do it in remembrance of the blood of thy Son, which was shed for them; that they may witness unto thee, O God, the Eternal Father, that they do always remember him."

I had heard and read those words thousands of times in my life. I had participated in lessons about what those words mean, and I thought I knew. In the prayer on the bread, we were being invited to remember Christ's life, His example of righteousness, His love, His character, His power, His condescension, and everything He did for us as we have learned it from the New Testament. In the prayer on the water, we were being invited to remember the Atonement He made for us—the amazing event that freed us from physical and spiritual death—again because of the New Testament account of those things.

But that day I realized there was much more to those words. Suddenly, my friend's words came back to me concerning her conversion, and I realized that remembering from the heart instead of the head isn't reserved only for investigators of the Church. I, too, can remember. My spirit once lived with God. He and others taught me there, and I saw Him and His Son. My spirit has memories within it that—even though a veil has been drawn—can and do surface if I let them.

If during the sacrament and times of prayer and meditation, I quiet my mind by disengaging it from the cares of life and reverently listen, my own spirit brings to my remembrance feelings and thoughts of what I once knew so well. I feel things my mind doesn't yet have words to express. These feelings lift and encourage and bring me closer to my Father in Heaven and my Savior. Instead of words that swim through my head, these feelings permeate to the very marrow of my bone with an intense warmth and joy.

During the Last Supper, Jesus was teaching the Apostles about the Father and explained that He is just like His Father and that if they knew Him, they would also know the Father (see John 14:7). At this point Philip asked the Savior to show them the Father. Jesus responded gently, repeating what He had said, "He that hath seen me hath seen the Father" (John 14:9), and then went on to tell Philip that he knows more than he thinks he knows. That is true for all of us. As Boyd K. Packer declared, "The Lord said in the Old Testament, and again to the Prophet Joseph Smith (Psalm 46:10 and D&C 101:16), 'Be still, and know that I am God.' There is such a thing as learning to listen spiritually. There is such a thing as having pure intelligence poured into the mind" (Boyd K. Packer, *The Holy Temple* [Salt Lake City: Bookcraft, 1980], 81). Often our hearts know more than our minds. But our minds are so busy that we can't hear our hearts speak.

Remembering isn't only about recalling what I have studied, read, or been taught in this life. My spirit has a memory, and when I am still and allow it to speak to me, I feel things that my mind doesn't originate. I know things my eyes and ears haven't physically perceived.

When I manage to "be still" and rest from the worries and cares of the world, then memories of God's love, His goodness, and His peace fill me. Knowledge about my Savior and Father in Heaven come back to me not in words but in feelings that strengthen and empower me to live the commandments more fully. When I am still, things that are part of my spirit move to my head and I remember. I attach to eternity. I am part of the peace, love, and joy that my spirit is accustomed to. I connect to the part of me that is God's.

# Gird Up Your Loins

*Ezra had prepared his heart to seek
the law of the Lord, and to do it, and to teach
in Israel statutes and judgments.*

Ezra 7:10

**However much faith to obey God we now have, we will
need to strengthen it continually and keep it refreshed
constantly. We can do that by deciding now to be more
quick to obey and more determined to endure. Learning
to start early and to be steady are the keys to spiritual
preparation. Procrastination and inconsistency are its
mortal enemies.**

Henry B. Eyring, "Spiritual Preparedness: Start Early and Be Steady,"
*Ensign,* Nov. 2005, 37

---

I love the phrase "gird up your loins" (D&C 43:19). In days of
old when people wore long robes, running (or just walking
fast) was difficult if not impossible. This is because the swift
movement causes a long robe to tangle around the ankles and
trip up the feet. Going up a hill or stairs is also difficult in long
robes. Feet can catch on the hem of the garment so that the
person steps on the robe and trips, and again the robe restricts
movement of the legs. Consequently, in biblical times, in order
to hurry, a person wearing long robes had to secure them so
that they didn't get in the way. To do this, a person would draw
the back bottom hem of the robe forward, pull the sides up and

tie them together so that it also secured the piece drawn up from the back. In essence it is a "diapering" effect. With the robes now "girded about the loins" and out of the way of the ankles and knees, the person was free to run or climb. Therefore, the phrase "gird up your loins" means to prepare to hurry forward. The key word here is *prepare.* Someone who hasn't *prepared* to move forward isn't going to get very far before his robes will entangle his legs, causing him to fall and possibly to suffer serious injury.

Likewise, we need to prepare to move forward spiritually. If we go about our days only performing the tasks of life, even if we do them honestly, we will miss our opportunities. It is like a young man who desires to be a professional football player but each day just lives—he sleeps, eats, works at his job, pays his bills, makes his bed, washes his dishes, and does the other maintenance chores of life. He does nothing bad, but at the same time he has done nothing that prepares him to play football. He hasn't learned the rules of the game. He hasn't exercised to strengthen his body and build endurance. He hasn't worked with the other members of the team and learned the specific plays. There is no way he is going to walk onto the field and be part of an NFL team. Even though he desired (and that desire might have been very intense) to be part of the team, he has not prepared to do so.

This is also true of celestial life. No one is going to accidentally arrive in the celestial kingdom. Executing the tasks of life so that we make it through each day isn't enough. Being righteous takes premeditated effort and preparation. As President Brigham Young said, "The men and women who desire to obtain seats in the celestial kingdom will find that they must battle every day" (Brigham Young, *Discourses of Brigham Young,* comp. John A.

Widtsoe [Salt Lake City: Deseret Book Co., 1954], 392).

I like to think of this in terms of our sports metaphor. Just as the athlete needs physical conditioning to be part of the team, you and I need spiritual conditioning to make it to the celestial kingdom. God has provided us with a great gift by providing the rules of play. Imagine what it would be like trying to play a game and no one gave you the rules. Imagine being on a football field, playing with all those players, and trying at that point to figure out the rules. Or imagine trying to win a tennis match while trying to follow the rules of basketball. Rules—the correct rules—have to be learned in quiet moments before the action begins.

Because He loves us so much and wants us to win, our Father in Heaven has provided a star player, who has shown us how to play the game perfectly. Jesus Christ never made a mistake. What athlete wouldn't love such a model? By studying and emulating Him, we can know exactly what to do. But that isn't all. We have a magnificent coach in the Holy Ghost. By heeding His instructions we can be assured of not just winning the game but executing each play correctly. We also have teammates, prophets, and other leaders who are instructing, helping develop team spirit, and coordinating teamwork so that we don't have to do it all by ourselves. Our task is to "gird up our loins" by consciously planning and preparing to play the game of life. As we make time in our day to learn the rules, study and follow the example of the "Star Player," and listen to the "Coach," we will be victorious in the game of life.

# Rejoice!

*I speak unto you these things that ye may rejoice,*
*and lift up your heads forever, because of the blessings*
*which the Lord God shall bestow upon your children.*

2 Nephi 9:3

**Find happiness in ordinary things, and keep your sense of humor.**

Boyd K. Packer, "Do Not Fear," *Ensign*, May 2004, 77

---

When we truly understand the good news that Jesus Christ has saved us from eternal misery, we can't help but rejoice. He lives! He loves us! He cares! Yet despite our knowledge of these truths, two of the adversary's most successful tools are discouragement and depression. Satan inserts all kinds of negative barbs into every good thought. It is almost as if there is a negative echo that accompanies every positive thought. "He lives!" and the echo, "So what?" "He loves us!" and the echo, "All those demands! You call that love?" "He cares!" and the echo, "But not about you. Why should he care about you? You're just one of a billion. How could He care about you?" When I hear these kinds of negative thoughts battling in my head, I find that one retort can silence them all. I just say, aloud if possible, "He died for me. What did you ever do for me?" There has never been an echo to that.

Jesus Christ knows us and He cares. The trick, then, is to silence the adversary, and the best way I've found to do that is to rejoice. Dismiss the "I'm not good enough" thoughts. Repent and then forget the sin. Push all the negative thoughts aside and rejoice that Jesus Christ has saved you.

Savor the good news, and dwell on all that is good. You have sickness, aches, and pains, but because of Jesus Christ these are only temporary. That is good news! You have family members or situations that disappoint you, but because of Jesus Christ those disappointments will be rectified. That is good news! People have cheated you, abused you, and unfairly taken advantage of you, but because of Jesus Christ there will be recompense. That is good news! People you love have died. You will too. But because of Jesus Christ you will live again. That is good news! There are people you have hurt. But because of Jesus Christ, they will be compensated and you will be forgiven if you sincerely repent. You have made major and minor mistakes. But because of Jesus Christ, if you learn to trust God and make better choices, your mistakes will be turned to work for your good. That is good news! You aren't as smart, or beautiful, or talented, or wealthy, or charming, or sociable as you want to be. But because of Jesus Christ you have sufficient for what you need to perform your labors in life. That is good news!

There isn't a negative thought you can think that doesn't have a positive counterpart because of Jesus Christ. So when a negative thought comes into your heart, chase it away by rejoicing. As Paul so aptly put it, "Rejoice in the Lord alway: and again I say, Rejoice" (Philip. 4:4).

President Hinckley encouraged, "In all of living have much of fun and laughter. Life is to be enjoyed, not just endured" (Gordon B. Hinckley, "Stand True and Faithful," *Ensign*, May 1996, 91). So develop a sense of humor. Let go of bad feelings and look for the good. Concentrate on the now and let the Lord take care of the rest. Carry a joyful song in your heart. Forget about yourself and let the Savior take care of you. Tend to the needs of others. Memorize a favorite verse of scripture to recite in order to drown out the negative echoes in your head. Savor the good memories as you forget the bad. Enjoy what you do. Love more. Be patient.

Does all that sound impossible? It is impossible, because Jesus Christ lives and loves us. That is the best news the world has ever known! All that is good is possible because of Him.

# Going Home

*I am the law, and the light. Look unto me, and
endure to the end, and ye shall live; for unto him that
endureth to the end will I give eternal life.*

3 Nephi 15:9

**I know that God lives, and I know that Jesus is the Christ,
our Savior and Redeemer. It is in the Shepherd's loving
arms and on His shoulders that we are carried home.**

Paul K. Sybrowsky, "If Christ Had My Opportunities . . . ", *Ensign,*  Nov. 2005, 35

It's amazing how something as simple as a scent can transport us through time. For example, when I smell hot cinnamon rolls, I'm back in my great-grandmother's little, white frame house. Or when I see cherries I'm in the orchard behind the green, shake-shingle house where I spent the first nine years of my life. Christmas lights send me on an absolute tailspin as decades of warm, wonderful memories flash through my mind. When these memories come, they seem to beckon me back to a place with a longing that is difficult to describe.

But as I've grown older, I've also discovered that going back is usually disappointing. My grandfather had a big front porch on his house with a curving, wide, brick wall capped with concrete, on both sides of the stairs. Those concrete caps were perfect slides. I remember as a child spending hours with my cousins sliding down, running back up, giggling, and sliding some more. We laughed and ran until we were exhausted. That porch with its stairs seemed like a giant playground. Recently, I was in southern Utah and drove by the house only to be startled by how small that porch and those concrete caps are.

You've probably had similar experiences. Time changes things. We change, and we see things differently. Sometimes that is sad, and other times it is a good thing. The reclusive old lady that lived in the stone house at the end of the street, no longer scares us. Instead, we feel empathy for her. The huge dog that seemed so menacing isn't around anymore, but we laugh to think how we used to walk the other way—the long way—around the block to avoid him.

Growing older and moving on has some advantages after all. And I'm sure that will be even more true as we leave this mortal life and return to our heavenly home. I'm sure we will take with us some warm, wonderful memories that we will savor forever. And I'm sure we will see many things in a new light and wonder why in the world we ever let them bother us.

Isaiah writes about this concept. At one point, he describes Satan's pride and haughtiness and how he brags that he will be higher than the stars of God and "will be like the most High" (Isa. 14:14). But despite his ego, Satan will be brought down to hell, and in the end those who look on him will gasp in disbelief, "Is this the man that made the earth to tremble, that did shake kingdoms?" (Isa. 14:16). We will probably think things like, "He doesn't even have a body! Why in the world did I ever let him influence me?"

When we finally go home, I'm certain we'll find there were many moments in our mortal life when we thought we were alone but weren't. The stories will be told, and we will weep as we learn that the angels and the Savior Himself always attended us, and that a loving Father always watched over us.

But the weeping and the joyful laughter won't last long, because there will be work to do—joyous work. And the things that seemed so important to us in this life will be insignificant, if even remembered, as we move forward in our eternal progression. As Elder Joseph B. Wirthlin said, "The gospel of Jesus Christ transcends mortality. Our work here is but a shadow of greater and unimaginable things to come" (Joseph B. Wirthlin, "The Virtue of Kindness," *Ensign*, May 2005, 28).

Once we have returned home, all that will matter is whether or not we put Jesus Christ first during our mortal life. At that point, there will be no doubt in our minds that Jesus Christ is the Good News.

Photograph courtesy of Carl M. Johnson

Sherrie Mills Johnson is the author of a historical novel, *A House with Wings,* and two adult nonfiction books, *Spiritually Centered Motherhood* and *Man, Woman, and Deity.* She authored *The Bible Treasury for LDS Children* and a series of twelve picture books on the Book of Mormon. Currently, she is having fun discussing gospel topics on her blog, Good News!, found at http://sherriejohnson.blogspot.com.

After raising her children, Sherrie returned to school and completed her bachelor's degree in English at Weber State University, her master's degree in English at Utah State University, and a doctorate in sociology at Brigham Young University. For the past ten years she has taught part-time in the Department of Ancient Scripture at Brigham Young University.

Married to Carl M. Johnson, Sherrie has ten children (nine daughters and one son) and 31 grandchildren (24 grandsons and 7 granddaughters).

Walnut Springs Press
110 South 800 West
Brigham City, Utah 84302
Http://walnutspringspress.blogspot.com

Copyright © 2009 by Sherrie Mills Johnson
All rights reserved. This book, or parts thereof, may
not be reproduced in any form without permission.

ISBN: 978-1-935217-34-3